For Claire —

Babe & the Kid

Babe & the Kid

The Legendary Story of Babe Ruth and Johnny Sylvester

Charlie Poekel

Foreword by Julia Ruth Stevens

Charleston   London

History
PRESS

Published by The History Press
Charleston, SC 29403
www.historypress.net

Copyright © 2007 by Charlie Poekel
All rights reserved

Cover design by Kenny Evans. Photos by Brett Wood and the *New York Daily News*.
Memorabilia courtesy of the Babe Ruth Museum and John Dale Sylvester Jr.

First published 2007

Manufactured in the United Kingdom

ISBN 978.1.59629.267.3

Library of Congress CIP data applied for.

To my wife Lynn,
whose inspiration and love created this book.

Contents

Foreword   9

Acknowledgements   13

Chapter One   15

Chapter Two   33

Chapter Three   81

Chapter Four   105

Chapter Five   119

Epilogue   139

Notes   145

Bibliography   149

Index   155

About the Author   159

Foreword

Kids—his own and everyone else's—were the delight of Daddy's life. Daddy loved children and children loved him. What made this amazing was the rough time that my father had in his own childhood. For eight years of his life, he lived at the St. Mary's Industrial School for Boys. What gave him the moral rectitude was the spirit and guidance of the Xaverian Brothers. And their spirit stayed with him all of his life.

Johnny Sylvester was a special friend of my dad's and his friendship lasted a lifetime. He was not a creation of the press. When my dad received the news of a boy in need of help, he responded. Of all the Yankees on the 1926 team, my dad was the one who wrote on a special baseball, "I'll knock a homer for you in Wednesday's game." This book tells what happened after he wrote those encouraging words to one very special eleven-year-old boy in Essex Fells, New Jersey.

The story as told in this book is incredible and should be an inspiration to everyone—young and old. My dad believed in young people. Throughout his life he, more than anyone else in the history of the United States, believed in young people.

On "Babe Ruth Day," my dad spoke of the need for young people to learn baseball. He said, "Baseball has to start with the young, for you cannot learn baseball when you are older."

When my dad was too ill to attend the funeral of Brother Gilbert, who was responsible for him entering baseball, he received an offer from a ten-year-old boy to attend in his place. My dad didn't hesitate when receiving the offer and allowed young Frank Haggerty of Danvers, Massachusetts, to represent him. No one linked the boys with the men more than my dad. As my dad related to boys, the boys related to my dad.

Julia Ruth Stevens, daughter of Babe Ruth, sitting with her father. *Courtesy of the Associated Press.*

Foreword

It is my foremost desire that this book will put forth the historical facts once and for all and be an everlasting tribute to a man whose likes we will never see again.

Julia Ruth Stevens

Acknowledgements

First and foremost I want to thank John Dale Sylvester Jr., who allowed me unlimited access to the Sylvester family records and his father's priceless scrapbook, which was started by an eleven-year-old boy living in Essex Fells, New Jersey. As Johnny never sought publicity for himself from his experiences with the great Babe Ruth, neither has his son or his family. But the Sylvesters recognize the importance of the story and the public's fascination with it for over eighty-one years.

Secondly, I want to thank Julia Ruth Stevens, who encouraged me to write the book and who through her stories and anecdotes about her father made the Great Bambino come alive for me.

And I want to thank all of the people who opened up their files and their resources for the research of this book. They came from various walks of life in order to complete the story. There were Bob Perna and Rick Hyer, tracing deeds of the Sylvester homes; Julie Bartlett, curator of the Calvin Coolidge Presidential Library & Museum, finding photographs; Molly Kodner, associate archivist at the Missouri Historical Society, locating the handwritten flight logs of Charles A. Lindbergh for his airmail routes between St. Louis and Chicago for October of 1926; Tracy Crocker, performing genealogical work on the Sylvester line; and Greg Schwalenberg, director of the Babe Ruth Museum in Baltimore, opening up the museum's display cases so that Brett Wood could photograph the prized Sylvester autographed baseballs.

And special thanks to those who used their time and their talents to bring this book about in the best possible light: Brett Wood, a great still-life photographer who spent hours photographing baseballs, the letters from Babe Ruth, Red Grange, Bill Tilden and others, along with the other treasures found in Johnny Sylvester's scrapbook; Kenny Evans, whose tremendous artistic talent and love of baseball resulted in the excellent cover and photographs; Doug Wyatt for obtaining the Sylvester patents; Laurie

Acknowledgements

Hoonhout McFeely from the Montclair-Kimberly Alumni Association; Ben Sakoguchi, who furnished his great artwork; Barrett Zinderman for doing what she does best: coordinating the talent and making things happen; Michael G. Bracey, who secured John Dale Sylvester's military records and deck logs from SC-520; Becky Redington, who ensured the high quality of the text formatting; and Chris Weston, who superbly formatted the images.

Many thanks to those who graciously consented to oral interviews: Ruth Elliott, who was there when the Babe walked through the door; John Dale Sylvester Jr., who is the custodian of his father's mementos; Robert Bush, who went to grammar school with Johnny Sylvester; Ted Keenan, who worked and sailed with Johnny; and Dan Bern, who spoke about the story and played his captivating song "Johnny Sylvester Comes Back to Visit the Babe" in his dressing room for me before appearing in Brooklyn, New York.

My appreciation also to Anne McCauley, Tim Cutting, Charles Stewart, Walter Giordano and Jean Giordano for furnishing research material. And to Tom Dawes and Rose Cali for their advice and suggestions.

And to the many unnamed individuals who work every day and perform such excellent work at the New York Public Library, the Boston Public Library, the Newark Public Library, Princeton University and the National Baseball Hall of Fame at Cooperstown, New York, who all helped me with my research.

And special thanks to my editors, Saunders Robinson, Doug Meyer and Hilary McCullough, and to all of the talented individuals at The History Press, especially art director Marshall Hudson, who helped bring this book to the public.

Chapter One

The year 1926 marked the 150th anniversary of the signing of the Declaration of Independence, and the country wanted to celebrate. In 1921, Philadelphia had been selected to host the Sesqui-Centennial Exposition. Louis Kahn, a world-renowned architect, was commissioned to be the chief designer. The exposition was going to be a mini world's fair, and it contained a giant stadium known as Philadelphia Municipal Stadium. The stadium had a classic 1920s style consisting of a horseshoe surrounding a track and football field with a seating capacity of over 110,000 people. The entrance to the exposition featured an eighty-foot-high Liberty Bell, the symbol of the fair, adorned with 26,000 fifteen-watt lights. Everyone entering the fair passed under the giant Liberty Bell. It was hoped that the French government would send over the *Mona Lisa* for the exposition, but the French feared it wouldn't be safe in a land where too much looting took place. When someone announced the painting "was the most famous masterpiece of French art," he was quickly told that it had been painted by an Italian.

The exposition also featured replicas of Mount Vernon, George Washington's Virginia homestead, as well as Sulgrave Manor, his English ancestral home. New Jersey's contribution was a stone replica of the Hessian barracks at Trenton during the Revolution.

The country was ready for the "greatest and gaudiest spree in its history," as F. Scott Fitzgerald had predicted, and it was about to witness one of the greatest years in all of sports history. It would become known as the "Golden Age of Sports," as America's athletes stood out in the country and the world as the greatest stars ever produced by a nation. They would topple old records and mark out new ones that still exist today. Golf in 1926 would witness a twenty-four-year-old Georgian named Bobby Jones win both the British and the U.S. Opens—the never-before-seen "double." Gene Tunney and Jack Dempsey would battle it out for heavyweight championship of the world before 120,000 eyewitnesses at Sesqui-Centennial Stadium. Red Grange, the "Galloping Ghost," would take his college exploits and bring the nation into professional football. "Big Bill" Tilden would show that an American could beat anyone from any country on the tennis courts. Gertrude Eberle, an eighteen-year-old girl from New York City, would become the first female to swim the English Channel and beat the record of the fastest man by two hours. And the king of the Golden Age would be George Herman "Babe" Ruth, whose seemingly unlimited number of home runs at the end of his Louisville Slugger galvanized the nation. In the words of sportswriter Tom Meany, the Babe "*was* the golden age."[1]

The year 1926 marked Babe Ruth's seventh year as a New York Yankee. Yankee Stadium, "the House that Ruth Built" in the Bronx, was three years old. The Babe was thirty-two years of age, and he was determined to get in shape and bring back the greatness that he had lost the year before. Ruth worked with Artie McGovern, his own personal trainer, at whose gym he spent four hours a day in a regimen that included weights, pulleys and quick action on a handball court to tone his reactions. By mid-January, Ruth had lost twenty-three pounds, his waist had shrunk from $48\frac{1}{2}$ to $39\frac{3}{4}$ inches and his neck size went from 17 to 16.[2]

Just to show off his well-muscled body, Ruth reported to spring training in St. Petersburg, Florida, on February 3—ahead of the rest of the team, which reported on March 3. Ruth felt good about himself, and he felt good about the Yankees. He had a prediction: "There is no doubt about it. The signs are unmistakable. The Yanks are going to win the pennant." Only one sportswriter, Fred Lieb, agreed with the Babe. Years later, Ruth would say, "Fred Lieb and I sure had our necks out on that one, but the team came through for us."[3] Most sportswriters felt that either Washington or Philadelphia would win the pennant. Famed sportswriter Westbrook Pegler was the most pessimistic of all the New York sportswriters, and his prediction was last place for the Yankees, the team that had finished seventh in 1925.

Just as Ruth was sure that the Yankees would win the pennant, there was another great hitter—who that year was serving as manager as well—Rogers Hornsby, "the Rajah," who was confident that the team he was playing on and managing—the St. Louis Cardinals—would win the pennant in the National League. Hornsby, a Texan, had replaced Branch Rickey as the field manager of the Cardinals. Baseball in the 1920s was the age of the player-managers. Besides Hornsby there were six others: Ty Cobb with the Detroit Tigers, Tris Speaker with the Cleveland Indians, Dave Bancroft

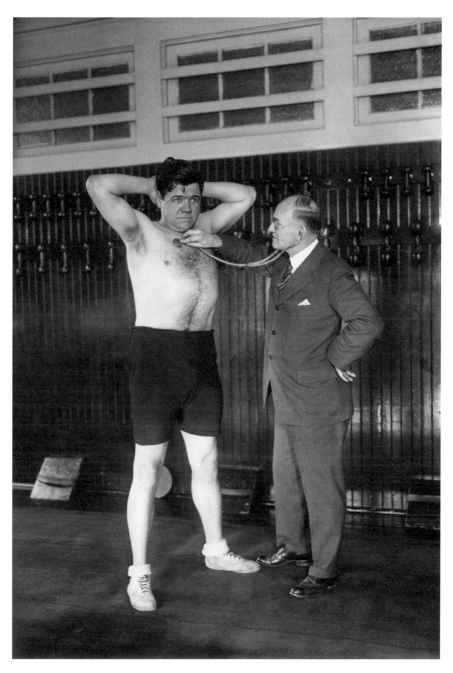

Babe Ruth being checked out by a doctor prior to the start of the 1926 baseball season. Over the winter, the Babe's physique had improved dramatically, largely due to his daily four-hour workout sessions with Artie McGovern at his gym in New York City. Ruth would repeat his winter conditioning at McGovern's for the next eight years. *Bettmann/CORBIS*.

Three members of Murderers' Row of the New York Yankees in 1926: Lou Gehrig, Babe
Ruth and Tony Lazzeri on the steps of the Yankee dugout. The year 1926 marked the
Babe's seventh year as a Yankee, first baseman Gehrig's first full year and Tony "Poosh 'Em

Up" Lazzeri's rookie year. The other members of Murderers' Row were Bob Meusel and Earle Combs. *The New York Public Library.*

with the Boston Braves, Eddie Collins with the Chicago White Sox, George Sisler with the St. Louis Browns and Bucky Harris with the Washington Senators. Hornsby was a blunt man who hated anyone who went to college and everyone knew he swore like a Texas trooper.

In the first address to his team at their spring training camp at Terell Wells, just outside of San Antonio, Hornsby presented his own version of what the Spanish conquistador Francisco Pizzaro had told his men, saying,

> *I want you fellows to listen to every word I am going to say. We are going to win this year's pennant. Don't go around telling everyone we're going to win. But we are going to win just the same. If there's anybody here who doesn't believe we are going to win, there's a train leaving for the north tonight and our secretary, Clarence Lloyd, will have a ticket for him. I'll trade away anyone who doesn't think we are going to win. If there's a man here who thinks we are a second division ball club, well, I just don't want him around.*[4]

The Yankee skipper in 1926 was the diminutive Miller Huggins. Huggins, a native of Cincinnati, was five foot, four inches and weighed only 146 pounds. He held a law degree, but his presence was needed at the ballpark—not the courtroom. After being a player and manager for the Cardinals for five seasons, Huggins became manager of the Yankees in 1918. He would constantly struggle with nervousness and headaches and gaining respect. He was once barred from a banquet, being told, "How can a little twerp runt like you be Babe Ruth's manager?" He would constantly strive to win the respect of his players and the fans, and in the end he did.

After spring training in St. Petersburg, the Yankees had a schedule of eighteen exhibition games. They won the first six and then beat the Dodgers in twelve consecutive games.

The season opened for the New York Yankees on April 14, 1926, in frigid Boston. It was a day not without added excitement for Ruth. Upon arriving in Massachusetts, he was told that there was an arrest warrant for him for failure to pay state income taxes. Ruth had a home in Sudbury, but he considered New York City to be his primary residence, and he had not filed Commonwealth of Massachussetts tax returns in either 1923 or 1924. Ruth immediately went to straighten the matter out with the commissioner of taxation at the statehouse in Boston, parking his car at Court Square. Ruth argued that his primary residence was New York and he simply maintained a summer house in Sudbury. While Ruth was inside making his arguments, a Boston policeman was ticketing his car outside. The end result was that the policeman withdrew the ticket, but Ruth had to pay the taxes.

Ruth then joined the team at Fenway Park, where he managed to hit two doubles, a single and steal a base. The Yankees, with Ruth igniting them, eked out a 12–11 win over the Red Sox and the 1926 season had begun.

Making his debut that cold day in Boston was the Yankee second baseman Anthony Lazzeri. Anthony "Tony" Lazzeri was from San Francisco and was the son of Italian immigrants. His father was a blacksmith. He was bantam-sized, weighing only 165 pounds, and he was an epileptic at a time when there were no drugs to control the condition. He had acquired the nickname of "Poosh 'Em Up Tony" while playing for Salt Lake City in the Pacific Coast League, where in 1925 he had "pushed up" 60 home runs and batted in 222 runs. Lazzeri would be part of a rookie Yankee infield. He would be teamed up with Mark Koenig at shortstop, who had only played twenty-five games with the Yanks in 1925, and with Lou Gehrig at first base, who was starting his first full season as a Yankee.

By the end of April, the Yankees had a record of 13–3 after an 8-game winning streak. On May 6, 1926, the *Sporting News* wrote, "[Manager] Miller Huggins has real 'Murderers' Row' with Ruth doing his part and aiding toward fine team spirit." This was the first time that the Ruth-centered Yankees would receive that appellation.[5] The *Sporting News* would mention "Murderers' Row" another five times in 1926, although the term is most closely associated with the 1927 Yankees. "Murderers' Row" consisted of Earle Combs, Lou Gehrig, Babe Ruth, Tony Lazzeri and Bob Meusel. In 1926, unlike future seasons, Gehrig would bat ahead of Ruth and Meusel would follow him.

Ruth hit four home runs in April and then eleven in May, including one on May 25 that is still considered the longest home run at Boston's Fenway Park. His shot that day traveled 512 feet horizontally and hit a bench in the bleachers forty-five rows from the bottom and five rows from the top.[6] By the end of May, the Yankees had a 16-game winning streak with a record of 30–9.

The 1926 season saw the Yankees' pitching staff rise to the top. Leading the staff was Herb Pennock, who finished the year with a record of 23–11 and an ERA of 3.62. Next came Urban Shocker, whose record was 19–11 with an ERA of 3.38. The third best pitcher was Waite Hoyt, who had a record of 16–2 with an ERA of 3.85.

Waite Hoyt had started his Major League career at age nineteen with the Boston Red Sox. It was with the Red Sox that Hoyt met Ruth and the two became lifelong friends. In their first encounter, Ruth looked at Hoyt and asked him, "Pretty young to be in the big league aren't you kid?" Hoyt's response was "Yep—same age you were when you came up, Babe."[7] Three

"To really know what sort of man Ruth was, you have to understand that his affection for children was sincere. The Babe, for all of his lusty living, for all of his bluff and often crude ways, had ever a soft spot in his heart for kids," wrote sportswriter Tom Meany. The Babe with kids near the bleachers at Yankee Stadium on April 22, 1926. *National Baseball Hall of Fame Library, Cooperstown, New York.*

members of the 1926 Yankees' team had played previously for the Boston Red Sox. Harry Frazee, owner of the Red Sox, sold Babe Ruth to the Yankees on January 3, 1920. In December of 1920, Frazee also sent Hoyt to the Yankees. And in 1923, Boston sent Herb Pennock to the Yankees. During the early 1920s, Hoyt supplemented his income by appearing in vaudeville, where he sang and told baseball stories. He also ventured in 1924 into the mortuary business and eventually opened a funeral home in Long Island. It didn't take long before he earned the nickname of the "Merry Mortician." One famous story about Hoyt had him driving a hearse to the Polo Grounds with a body in it, pitching a game and then delivering the putrefying corpse to his father-in-law's funeral home in Brooklyn.[8]

The Cardinals solidified their team midway through the season. In a trade on June 14 with John McGraw of the New York Giants, one that was later referred to as McGraw's worst trade, the Cardinals obtained Billy Southworth for Heine Mueller. Mueller would have a mediocre season with the Giants but Southworth, the pride of Harvard, Nebraska, would be energized by the Cardinals' quest for the pennant and bat .329 for the season and play exceptionally well in right field.

Eight days after the trade, the Cardinals made another brilliant move in the acquisition of veteran pitcher Grover Cleveland Alexander when Joe McCarthy of the Chicago Cubs put him on waivers. Alexander had suffered a broken ankle in spring training and had been institutionalized the winter before for his alcoholism. McCarthy felt that Alexander was too much of an alcoholic and that his best pitching days were over. Hornsby was able to pick up Ol' Pete for the paltry sum of $4,000. Hornsby would say later about Alexander, "He had the greatest control I've ever seen. He could almost nick the corners of a soft-drink bottle cap." Hornsby, the player-manager, asked Branch Rickey, the general manager, to claim Alexander. He wanted him on his team even though he had heard that Ol' Pete carried a gin bottle more often than a glove. And he wasn't an impressive looking man. One biographer wrote, "You could stand Grover Cleveland Alexander among a group of farm laborers and he would blend in."[9] In his first appearance as a Cardinal that year, Alexander faced his former Cubs' teammates and pitched a four hitter, winning the game 3–2. After the game, Alexander tipped his hat, which was always too small for him, to McCarthy.

During 1926, Ruth continued helping children and children's causes. Reverend E.J. Flanagan, founder of Father Flanagan's Boys' Home, announced on June 13 that Ruth had joined Father Flanagan's campaign to end profiteering in homeless boys. Ruth wrote Father Flanagan that he was "all for the boys and takes a deep interest in them."[10] This publicity

The Cardinals' veteran pitcher Grover Cleveland "Ol' Pete" Alexander, age thirty-nine, as he appeared in action on September 9, 1926. Let go by the Cubs in June 1926 because they thought he was finished, Alexander would shine for the Cardinals and become their World Series hero. His control as a pitcher was so good that in the 1920s, Cubs' catcher Bill Kellefer would hold a tomato can behind home plate and Ol' Pete would fire a ball into it every time. *Associated Press/Wide World.*

was good for Ruth, especially since it followed by one day reports of Ruth being arrested for fishing without a license in Michigan on June 11, five days before the season opened.[11] Although an arrest warrant was issued, the press was quick to point out that the Babe's catch was reported to have been "only a few scrawny bluegills."[12]

While Yankee pitcher Waite Hoyt was known as the "Merry Mortician," left-handed Herb Jeffries Pennock was known as the "Knight of Kennett Square." He had an estate in Kennett Square, Pennsylvania, where he raised silver foxes and headed fox hunts. Ruth would often be a guest of Pennock's at Kennett Square and would remark that riding horses after a bunch of foxes was harder than it looked.

In July of 1926, Pennock was being honored by his hometown, and after a game in Philadelphia, he invited Waite Hoyt, Joe Dugan and Babe Ruth to accompany him to Kennett Square. The four Yankees were featured at a parade and a dinner. After dinner the Yankee players attended a street fair that had been set up as part of the celebration. At the fair there was a booth where you could win prizes by throwing balls. The Yankees went wild at throwing the lightweight balls and ended up winning almost all the prizes in the booth. Hoyt in particular couldn't stop tossing the balls; he started throwing curves and knuckleballs to hit the targets. At the end of the street fair episode, Babe and his teammates returned most of the prizes to the distraught street fair barker. All was not good, however, as Hoyt had severely injured his pitching arm. The next day he told Miller Huggins that it had happened during a game. One doctor examined Hoyt's arm and said he would be out for the rest of the season. Huggins, however, had Hoyt go to Rochester, New York, where Doc Knight, a famous sports bonesetter, worked on Hoyt's arm and had him back in shape in about three weeks.

Besides seeing greatness in sports, the Roaring Twenties also saw unbridled frivolities. On July 23, 1926, the Babe took time off for a publicity event to aid the Citizens' Military Training Camps. He donned an army uniform and attempted to catch a baseball dropped from an airplane at Mitchell Field in Long Island. The army plane took off and dropped a ball at one thousand feet, but the exhaust from the propellers carried the ball beyond the field. Five more balls were dropped with the Babe desperately trying to get under them, all the time in grueling heat. On the seventh attempt, the plane dropped to three hundred feet and, according to the *New York Times* account, Ruth "steadied himself and neatly caught it." Ruth had set another world record. The new record didn't impress Yankees' owner Colonel Rupert, who told Ruth, "No more of that. Play ball in the ballpark."[13]

The Associated Press reported on August 30, 1926, that Ruth had signed a $100,000 contract for a twelve-week tour over the Pantages Western vaudeville circuit to start after the end of the World Series. Agents for Pantages said it was the largest contract of its kind ever signed in vaudeville, as the Bambino would make the tour alone. The tour was scheduled to open in Minneapolis and would take Ruth to the Pacific Coast.

As the Cardinals battled for domination in the National League, they relied more and more on their ace thirty-nine-year-old pitcher, Grover Cleveland Alexander. Alexander had been born near Elba, Nebraska, on February 26, 1887, and was named for President Grover Cleveland, who was in office at his birth. Some referred to him as "Alexander the Great," but most referred to him as "Ol' Pete." Since coming to the Cardinals in June of 1926, Ol' Pete had secured sixteen wins for the Cardinals. In fact, on September 5 some two thousand fans traveled from St. Louis to Cincinnati to watch Alexander pitch the Cardinals into first place. Always wearing a cap that was too small and to the side, Alexander looked unassuming, but as Richard Vidmer pointed out in the *Times*, "His control over the ball is as great as Mussolini's over Italy."[14] For three years in a row, he had won over thirty games in a season.

The race for the pennant in the National League was between the Red Legs, the Pirates and the Cardinals. The Red Legs held first place from mid-May until July. Then the Pirates, the 1925 world champions, took the lead for a month, until on August 31 the Cardinals obtained the top berth.

On Friday, September 24, 1926, the Cardinals won the pennant by a 6–4 win over the Giants in New York. Fifty loudspeakers had been placed in St. Louis's business district. At game's end, there was a huge celebration in the streets where thousands blew horns, created any noise they could and paraded through the streets. The *Sporting News* reported that "perhaps no city in the country ever experienced a more spontaneous and lasting demonstration over a baseball victory."[15] The Cardinals won their first National League championship in fifty years—the last St. Louis championship of any kind had been in 1888, when the St. Louis Browns of Charles Camiskey and Arlie Latham won their final AA pennant. Hornsby, distracted by his managerial duties, had his batting average fall to .317

For the Cardinals it had been a stellar regular season: first baseman "Sunny Jim" Bottomley led the National League in doubles with 40 and RBIs with 120, and he knocked in 19 home runs; third baseman Les Bell drove in 10 runs and hit .325 and had a slugging percentage of .518; MVP catcher Bob O'Farrell hit .293 with 30 doubles and 7 home runs; Flint Rhem tied for the league lead at 20 wins and finished the season with an ERA of 3.21; Bill Sherdel went 16–12; veteran Jesse Haines went 13–4; and Grover Cleveland Alexander went 9–7 in a relief/spot-starting role.

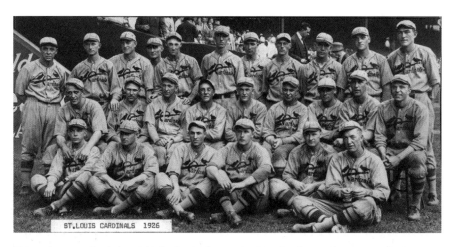

Team photograph of the 1926 St. Louis Cardinals. The Cardinals clinched the National League pennant on September 24, 1926, in a game against the New York Giants in New York. *National Baseball Hall of Fame Library, Cooperstown, New York.*

The Indians made a late charge in September and Babe's final three home runs came when they were needed most. The Yankees were playing the St. Louis Browns in St. Louis for a double-header. Battling Cleveland, the Yanks needed to win. To make matters worse, the night before the double-header the Yankees' players received little or no sleep. But they weren't out partying; hundreds of Cardinals' fans had been up the night before celebrating the Cards clinching the pennant. The fans stormed the Chase Hotel, where the Yankees were staying, and banged on pot lids, set off firecrackers and threw all sorts of garbage at the windows of the rooms of the Yankees' players. In spite of the late-night distractions, the next day the Yankees swept both games from the Browns. During those two games, Ruth hit three home runs, a double, a single and walked three times. The Yankees ended up winning the pennant by 3 games, with a record of 91–63.

The 1926 season was great for the Babe. He ended the season with 47 home runs (the second-place finisher had 19), batted .372 and drove in 155 runs. He led the league in walks (144), runs scored (139), total bases and slugging percentage (737). He had played practically every game. For some reason, he did not receive the MVP award that year; it went to George Burns of the second-place Cleveland Indians instead. Gehrig led all American League hitters in triples (20), scored 135 runs and hit 47 doubles. Earle Combs hit .299 with 12 triples and 113 runs batted in.

As poetic justice would have it, the Yankees won their pennant in the city of St. Louis on September 25, 1926, by beating the St. Louis Browns in a

Babe Ruth smiling after the Yankees won the pennant on September 25, 1926. During the 1926 season, Ruth hit forty-seven home runs. The next highest batter in baseball hit twenty-one. This started Ruth's seven-year streak of hitting more than forty home runs in a season—a record that has yet to be broken. *Bettmann/CORBIS.*

Team photograph of the 1926 New York Yankees. The Yankees won the pennant that year with a record of 97–63, clinching it in St. Louis after winning both games of a double-header with the Browns. *National Baseball Hall of Fame Library, Cooperstown, New York.*

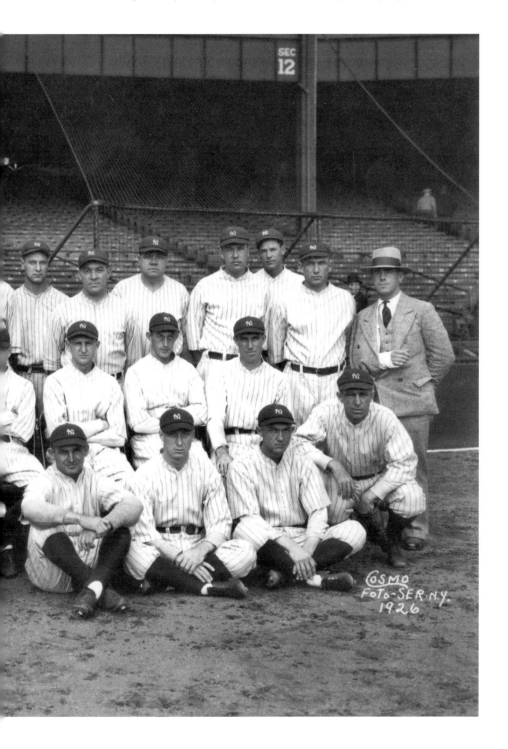

double-header, while the Cardinals clinched their division in New York by beating the New York Giants.

During the last week of September, Rogers Hornsby received a telegram that read, "Your mother sinking fast. You cannot possibly reach here to see her alive. Her dying wish is that you remain for the Series."[16] Mary Dallas Rogers Hornsby had been an invalid for the past twelve years, but she had enthusiastically followed the exploits of her son. Her son's Christian name was derived from his mother's maiden name. On September 29, she passed away at age sixty-three, and as was her wish, her son remained in New York.

Chapter Two

I'll knock a homer for you in Wednesday's game.
—Babe Ruth

John Dale Sylvester was born in Caldwell, New Jersey, on April 5, 1915. He was the son of Horace Clapp Sylvester Jr. and Helen Keenan. He had one sister, Ruth, who was born on September 26, 1920, and two brothers: Horace Clapp Sylvester III, born on November 25, 1912, and Peter Leroy Sylvester, born on February 11, 1925.

Ancestors of the Sylvesters arrived in North America in 1630 from Somerset, England. The family was related to Nathaniel Sylvester, who was one of the founders of Shelter Island, New York. Nathaniel had journeyed from England to Barbados, and then to Shelter Island. His grand manor house was known as Sylvester Manor; it was rebuilt and still stands on Shelter Island.

Johnny's paternal grandfather was Horace Clapp Sylvester. He was born in Westminster, Vermont, in 1840. When the Civil War broke out, he enlisted and was wounded at the Battle of Antietam, after which he served as a confidential secretary in the War Department. When the war was over, he became a dry goods merchant in Brooklyn, New York. He also became a partner at one time with A.T. Stewart & Company. He died in 1911.

Horace Clapp Sylvester Jr. was born in 1884 in New York City. He grew up in Montclair, New Jersey, and attended Montclair High School. After graduating from Montclair High School, Horace began his career with N.W. Halsey & Co. in New York City. He started in December of 1901 as an office boy earning three dollars per week. He worked his way up through every department, becoming assistant manager of the municipal bond department in 1912 and manager in 1914. In 1916, the Halsey firm was absorbed by the National City Company, a securities affiliate of the National City Bank. Horace became head of the municipal department and in 1926 became a vice-president of National City Company.

Home of Horace C. Sylvester Jr. and his family, located between Roseland Avenue and Wootton Road in Essex Fells, New Jersey. The Sylvester family had moved to this home in 1921 from Caldwell, New Jersey, and on October 11, 1926, Babe Ruth came to the house to pay a visit to a recovering eleven-year-old Johnny Sylvester. *Courtesy of St. Peter's Episcopal Church, Essex Fells, New Jersey.*

After spending his early years in Caldwell, New Jersey, Johnny and his family moved to the adjoining town of Essex Fells in 1921, moving into a large sprawling house located between Roseland Avenue and Wootton Road. Essex Fells, New Jersey, lies approximately nineteen miles due west from New York City and is nestled in the second mountain range. The name of the small borough results from being in Essex County and from "Fells," which is either from John Fell, one of the original developers, or from the English name for a small hill.

In Essex Fells, Johnny attended the Essex Fells Grammar School and played baseball. He was known as the "Babe Ruth kid" at the school because of his strong hitting ability. The young boy was an enthusiastic fan of the New York Yankees and, like almost all of the boys his age, his idol was Babe Ruth.

Toward the end of the summer of 1926, Horace Sylvester and his family rented a house in Bay Head, New Jersey. Bay Head is located on the Jersey Shore on the peninsula that separates Barnegat Bay from the Atlantic Ocean. It lies about seventy miles south of New York City. It was originally established by the Bayhead Land Company, but due to a sign maker's misspelling it became known as "Bay Head."

One of the many activities for Horace's young son Johnny that summer was horseback riding. One day toward dusk, when Johnny was riding a horse with a group of friends and heading back to the stables, Johnny's horse stepped into a hole and both horse and rider fell to the ground. The horse got up first and then kicked Johnny in the head. For the rest of the summer, Johnny suffered from the injury. The injuries to Johnny got progressively worse, and by the end of September he was quite seriously ill and in danger of dying.

Young Johnny was diagnosed with osteomyelitis—a deterioration of the bones due to inflammation. It can occur anywhere in the body, and for Johnny it was in his head. Doctors questioned whether he would live. The condition made Johnny extremely lethargic and depressed. He didn't feel like doing anything and was confined to his bed.

Just two years earlier, Calvin Coolidge Jr., the sixteen-year-old son of President Calvin Coolidge, had gotten a blister on his big toe while playing tennis without wearing socks. The blister became infected, and the young boy developed blood poisoning. When doctors at Walter Reed Army Hospital opened up his leg to drain the blood, they noticed that the boy was suffering from osteomyelitis. Young Calvin Coolidge Jr. died a few days later.

Years in the future, Yankee great Mickey Mantle injured his left shin during a football game in 1946 when he was a sophomore in high school.

Calvin Coolidge with his sons, Calvin Coolidge Jr. and John Coolidge, throwing a baseball. In July of 1924, after playing tennis with his brother on the White House tennis courts, Calvin Coolidge Jr. contracted an infection and died within two weeks. He was sixteen years old. *The Calvin Coolidge Presidential Museum and Home.*

As his injury swelled, he developed osteomyelitis. When doctors said his leg might have to he amputated, his mother took him to Crippled Children's Hospital in Oklahoma City, where he was treated with doses of penicillin every three hours around the clock. His leg was saved.

In the year 1926, Fleming's discovery of the penicillin bacterium was still two years away, and it would be several more years before antibiotics were in use.

Erroneous reports of Johnny's medical problems would include "sinus condition," as reported in the *New York Times*; "spinal fusion," as reported in the *New York World*; "back problem," as written in *The Babe Ruth Story*; "blood poisoning," as written in *Time* magazine; and "crippled by bone disease," as written by author Lois P. Nicholson.

By the beginning of the 1926 World Series in October, Johnny was in real danger of dying. According to Johnny's mother, physicians said that Johnny had about a week to live.

As the 1920s were the Golden Age of Sports, they were also the Golden Age of Sportswriters. Jack Lang, the prizewinning New York journalist, described the Golden Age of Sportswriting best:

> As far as history's sake, the giants of this industry were working in the Twenties. Back then the writer had a chance to elaborate. Writers waxed poetic five or six paragraphs before they even told you who was playing. Sometimes you didn't get the scores until the fifteenth or sixteenth paragraphs. They described the weather, the stadium, the crowd—which you couldn't get by with today. Back then the only way people got their sports was through the newspaper.

At the top of the list of the great sportswriters of the Golden Age was Damon Runyon. Born Alfred Damon Runyon, he shortened it to Damon Runyon, feeling that only Protestants had triple names. He would later be forever known for his theatrical creation *Guys and Dolls*, but for twenty-five years before that he covered the World Series as a sportswriter.

This is how Runyon on October 1, 1926, sized up the forthcoming Cardinals-Yankees showdown:

> The World Series of 1926 is of unusual interest if only because it presents on the same bill the two greatest baseball headliners of these times.
>
> They are Mr. George Herman Babe Ruth, sometimes called the Big Bam (Oh Mister Printer, PLEASE don't make that bum) and Rogers Hornsby, the former Home Run King, and the latter probably the greatest right-handed hitter of all time.
>
> Mr. George Herman Babe Ruth would seem to be entering the series with something of an advantage over his opponent in the matter of batting condition, Mr. Ruth being in the proverbial pink, while Rogers Hornsby has just closed one of the leanest seasons of his career because of illness. Mr. Ruth hit around .369 in the year and nudged out some forty-seven home runs, so you can see he was feeling first rate all year.
>
> Rogers Hornsby, on the other hand, got so far away from the .300 mark that he felt positively naked. He wound up less than a score of points beyond .300, which is little more than infield batting practice to Rogers Hornsby. However, he may get going in the series and knock the boys bowlegged. You can't keep a squirrel on the ground.
>
> Mr. Ruth and Rogers Hornsby undoubtedly represent the greatest amount of pounding power that baseball has ever known. I mean to say they hit the ball harder than any batsmen that ever lived.

The Bambino and the Rajah. Babe Ruth, one of baseball's greatest left-handed hitters, with Rogers Hornsby, one of baseball's greatest right-handed hitters, together before the start of game three of the 1926 World Series at Sportsman's Park, St. Louis, on October 5, 1926. Ruth had an outstanding batting average of .372 during the regular season, while Hornsby was distracted by illness and his duties as player-manager and had his least productive season since 1919, with a season average of .317. *Bettmann/CORBIS.*

If you could combine their batting power into one punch it would probably be sufficient to drive a baseball from the Battery to the Bronx, which is quite a distance.

Of the two, I believe Rogers Hornsby hits the ball harder, and Mr. Ruth hits it farther. This seems contradictory, but I can explain it. Rogers Hornsby hits the ball on the beeper or nose, with a straightaway drive. It shoots from his bat like a rifle bullet, traveling in a straight line.

Mr. Ruth, as a rule, hits under the ball, lifting it when he connects as a golfer lifts a golf ball. Rogers Hornsby seems to always be trying to break the infielders' kneecaps, while Mr. Ruth seems to be firing at the landscapes beyond the walls. They both get the same general result, which are additions to their batting averages.

In their meetings in the World Series, Mr. Ruth will have the inconsiderable advantage over Rogers Hornsby of absence of responsibility, other than that which pertains to playing the outfield and making home runs at stated intervals. Rogers Hornsby will be playing second base and managing his club at the same time. However, I seem to remember that the responsibilities thus involved did not keep the Washington club under Stanley Harris from winning the World Series of 1924 from the Giants under the great John McGraw, whose only responsibility was sitting on the fence. [17]

As the World Series approached, it was pointed out that the Cardinals were on the average a slightly younger team than the Yankees. Thirteen of the Cardinals' players had been born in the twentieth century, while this was true of only eight Yankees. The Cardinals also had the youngest player in Edgar Clough, who was nineteen. Tony Lazzeri, at age twenty-one, was the youngest of the Yankees' players. Babe Ruth was the tallest and heaviest member of either team at six foot three inches, with a weight of 215 pounds.

A little after 11:00 a.m. on Saturday, October 2, 1926, a man arrived at Yankee Stadium wearing a brown suit that bordered on plum and a brown silk shirt over his costly silk BVDs. He was one of the first players to arrive. His name was Babe Ruth, and when he put on the Yankees' home pinstripe uniform, although it bore neither his name nor a number, there wouldn't be a soul at Yankee Stadium that day who didn't recognize him.

By 1:30 p.m., over sixty-three thousand fans had jammed Yankee Stadium in the Bronx, New York, for game one of the 1926 World Series. Yankee Stadium was sparkling new, having been opened just three years before. One sportswriter said, "It loomed up like the great Pyramid of Cheops

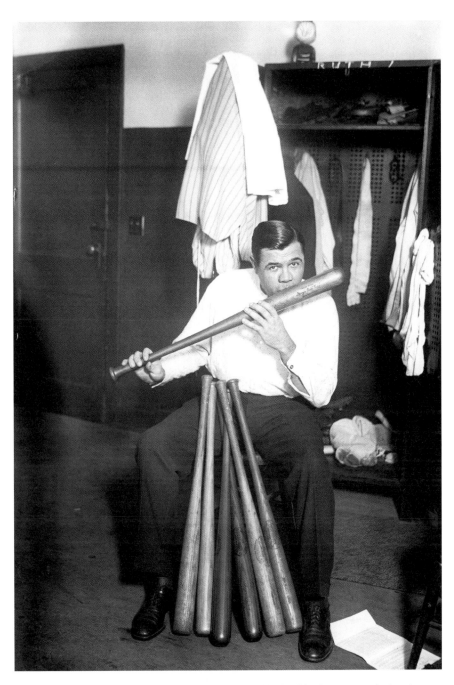

The Babe kissing one of his bats that hopefully would bring him home runs during the 1926 World Series between the Yankees and the Cardinals. Although the press reported that Ruth's bats weighed as much as fifty-two ounces, he never used a bat heavier than forty-two ounces, and as his career unfolded he went to lighter and lighter bats. *Bettmann/ CORBIS.*

from the sands of Egypt." It was the country's first triple-decked ballpark and the only one to be called a stadium. Ten thousand other fans gathered in downtown New York near city hall to follow the progress of the game on two giant scoreboards that were set up for the occasion. Over two hundred extra New York City policemen were on hand to handle the crowds.

In St. Louis, loudspeakers were placed in downtown locations to bring the game to the fans in the street. The city's chamber of commerce installed a radio in its large dining room on its eighth floor and announced that it would be on for all of the games and invited all of its members to come and listen.[18] The Odeon Theatre said it would have play-by-play recreations on its movie screen, and the Liberty Music Hall advertised that fans could come to its movie house to see the "World's Largest Electric Baseball Playboard," which was a new invention "guaranteed to be as good as a box seat in New York or St. Louis ballparks."[19] Newsboys had megaphones and were ready to repeat what the radio broadcast. And at noon St. Louis time, half an hour before the first game was to begin in New York, 120 members of the musicians' union paraded through the downtown area, warming up the fans by playing songwriter Ray Henderson's newest hit "Bye, Bye Blackbird," which the St. Louis fans turned into "Bye, Bye Yankees!"

In Essex Fells, New Jersey, bedridden Johnny Sylvester listened to the game on the radio. The *New York Times* estimated that the ratio of radio listeners to stadium attendees would be 250 to 1, and thus Johnny was one of 15 million people to hear the game as it was broadcast over WEAF, WJZ and twenty-three other radio stations in the United States and Canada. Graham McNamee, a former concert singer turned announcer, gave the country's listeners his own exciting play-by-play description of the game. The Motor Electric Company in St. Louis advertised $79 radios to anyone who could make a $15 deposit and then monthly payments of $10 with no interest until the purchase was paid off. Radio sales throughout the country were on the rise, and the following year would see sales hitting $425 million.

Game day was overcast and misty at game time, with a soggy natural grass field awaiting the players at Yankee Stadium.

Senate nominee Robert F. Wagner committed the first error of the day when he dropped the ceremonial first pitch, thrown to him by Colonel Jacob Ruppert, the Yankees' owner. Besides Wagner, the field box seats were full of celebrities. Next to Wagner sat New York City Mayor Jimmy Walker, impeccably dressed wearing his familiar derby. Walker had become mayor earlier that year and was a "slim, sharp-featured, nap-brim fedora type who could fashion a wisecrack in a trice, could charm an enemy, on a friend, or silence a heckler with a deft ad lib, who looked like the valedictorian of a Catholic high-school graduating class, sounded like a born New Yorker, and

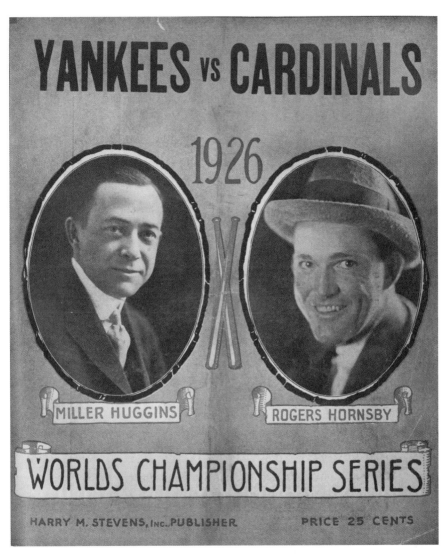

The official program of the 1926 World Series, published by Harry M. Stevens. Stevens was an immigrant salesman from Ohio who pioneered the use of a roster to help fans tell who the players were. He added a score card for them to complete as the game progressed. He also held the food concessions in ballparks nationwide. During the 1920s, he introduced the idea of putting straws in soda bottles so that the fans could watch a game and drink at the same time. *Author's Collection.*

comported himself like a vaudeville hoofer."[20] Behind Wagner and Walker sat former heavyweight champion of the world Jack Dempsey. Dempsey had been dethroned the previous month in Philadelphia when a young Irish fighter, John Eugene Tunney from Greenwich Village, the fighting marine, had beaten him for the title at Sesqui-Centennial Stadium in Philadelphia.

Also in attendance were two of the biggest sports magnates of the day—George "Tex" Rickard and Charles C. "Cash and Carry" Pyle. Rickard had been a gold miner, saloonkeeper and gambling hall operator who took to promoting prizefighting. He discovered William Harrison "Jack" Dempsey—who came from Manassa, Colorado, and became known as "the Manassa Mauler"—and maintained a lifelong friendship with him. The month before, Rickard had promoted the heavyweight championship bout in Philadelphia where Dempsey lost the title to Gene Tunney. Dempsey, despite losing his crown, continued to be the country's favorite brawler by stating that when his stunning movie star wife Estelle asked him what had happened, he told her, "I forgot to duck."

Charles C. "Cash and Carry" Pyle was born in Delaware, Ohio, the son of a Methodist minister. Although his mother wanted him to become a preacher as well, Pyle was more interested in promoting. Pyle became the owner of a chain of movie theaters, but in 1925 his life changed dramatically when he met Illinois football star Red Grange and became his agent, becoming the first player agent in sports history. Pyle took Grange from playing as an amateur to playing as a professional. Grange would later comment that Pyle was more interested in promoting himself than earning money, and he would tip porters on the Pennsylvania railroad ten dollars if they mentioned his name in public and ten cents if they didn't.

At Yankee Stadium that day, Pyle would make quite a scene at six feet, 190 pounds, dressed in spats, sporting a moustache and carrying a cane. Pyle was present at the stadium that day with amateur tennis stars Suzanne Lenglen and Vincent Richards. He was in the process of turning two of the greatest amateur tennis players in the world into professionals. Lenglen was the French-born female tennis ace who the *New York Times* called the "greatest female player that ever lived," and the *London Times* said that she made "Wimbledon the greatest tournament in the world." She appeared at the game wearing an attractive beige suit and afterward said she had learned very little about how baseball is played, but she promised to do so before the end of the series. Vincent Richards was a protégé of "Big" Bill Tilden, who he teamed up with in 1918 to win the United States doubles championship at age fifteen; to this day, Richards remains the youngest male ever to have won a major tournament. Both Lenglen and Richards would usher in professional tennis the following evening at an event sponsored by Pyle at Madison Square Garden that would draw thirteen thousand spectators.

The series had international attention, as the *New York Times* reported also that "for the first time in history" the French press and public were following the World Series and that the papers in Paris had devoted space to the respective merits of the Cardinals and the Yankees.

At the stadium that day, fans bought the program published by Harry M. Stevens, who invented the score card and would hold the food concessions at baseball parks throughout the country until 1994. Vendors would call out, "You can't tell the players without a score card!" And they were right. At that time, the uniforms of the players did not have their names or numbers on them. There was no public address system in use. So unless the spectators could tell the players from sight, the roster and score card contained within the program were essential.

The game's starting pitchers were "Wee Willie" (although he stood five foot, ten inches) Sherdel, who had won sixteen games and lost only two for the Cardinals during the regular season, and lean and lanky Herbert J. "Herb" Pennock, who had won twenty-three games for the Yankees in 1926. Both pitchers were southpaws, but Pennock had the experience of previously pitching in a World Series game, while this would be Sherdel's debut in the fall classic.

The Cardinals were the first to score when, in the top of the first, Taylor Douthit, who had hit .317 during the regular season, knocked a double to right and then scored on a single by Jim Bottomley, the Cardinals' first baseman. Bottomley was from Nokomis, Illinois, and he was one of the first to be brought up to the Cardinals through Branch Rickey's farm system. In his first season with the Cardinals in 1923, Bottomley hit .371, and in 1924 he set a Major League record when he drove in twelve runs in one game, hitting three singles, a double and two home runs. This record of 12 RBIs in a single game has never been broken and was only equaled in 1993 by Mark Whitten of the St. Louis Cardinals. Because of his constant smile, Bottomley was known as "Sunny Jim."

In the bottom of the first inning, Sherdel gave up a walk to Earle Combs on four straight pitches, and then he walked Ruth after Koenig flied out. Bob Meusel walked. With the bases loaded, up came the Yankees' first baseman Lou Gehrig, making his first World Series appearance at the plate. He hit sharply to Thevenow, the Cardinals' shortstop, who fired to Hornsby at second, who then made a wide throw to Bottomley at first. Combs scored the first Yankees' run, and Gehrig was safe at first with his first World Series RBI.

In the third inning, Babe Ruth did the unexpected. After hitting a single, he was moved to second base by a bunt, and in the process he split his pants. Play-by-play announcer Graham McNee relayed that "Ruth is the color of a red brick house." Doc Woods, the Yankees' trainer, rushed to Ruth's side with a needle and thread and sewed a patch, using a piece of the ground tarpaulin that Yankees' groundskeeper Phil Schenck had cut out.

The bats of both the Yankees and the Cardinals were silent as the game became a real pitchers' duel and remained tied at 1–1 until the sixth inning.

In the bottom of the sixth, Ruth singled and then Meusel bunted him to second. Lou Gehrig then knocked home the go-ahead run with a sharp single to right. Lazzeri then lined a shot to left and Gehrig, who hesitated, tried to get to third and was tagged out.

The Yankees hung on and beat the Cardinals 2–1 in a swiftly played game that took just one hour and forty-eight minutes to complete. Gehrig was credited with driving in the game's winning run—a feat he would perform an astonishing eight times in his baseball career.

A gorgeous summer day brought a balmy southwest breeze to the Bronx on Sunday, October 3, for game two. Over 65,000 fans showed up to make the gate the biggest in World Series history. Fans had started lining up at 5:00 a.m., and the last bleacher seat was sold before noon. Over 4,000 fans had to be turned away. A police detail of 335 men arrived at 8:00 a.m. to keep order. Of the gatecrashers who tried to get in, 19 were "personal friends" of Colonel Jacob Ruppert, the Yankees' owner, and 11 were "relatives" of Gene Tunney. Three men were arrested for selling illegal and exorbitantly priced tickets when they sold $5.50 sets for $20.00 to plainclothes detectives. The band at the stadium played "Hail, Hail the Gang's All Here" for the Cardinals and "The Sidewalks of New York" for the Yankees, or Hugmen, as they were called in the press after their diminutive but popular manager.

The Cardinals sent to the mound the veteran thirty-nine-year-old Grover Cleveland Alexander, who Richard Vidmer of the *New York Times* said was "a grizzled gray-haired pitcher who was called 'The Great' when Ruth was a rookie, Lazzeri a schoolboy and Koenig was peddling papers on the streets of San Francisco."[21]

The Yankees' pitcher was "Old Red Neck" Urban Shocker, the former star of the St. Louis Browns. Shocker, born Urbain Shockor, had changed the spelling of his names for the benefit of the sportswriters. He was one of seventeen Major League pitchers whose spitball was "grandfathered" as a legal pitch after spitballs were outlawed in 1920. Shocker had won nineteen games for the Yankees in 1926, but at the end of the season he had three straight defeats.

Alexander got off to an inauspicious start when Meusel, Lazzeri and Dugan hit singles, scoring two runs, and he made a wild throw during a double steal. But after that rough start, Ol' Pete settled down and actually became stronger as the game progressed. After allowing a single by Earle Combs in the third inning, Alexander put down the next twenty-one Yankee batters in order, striking out ten.

In the ninth inning, the Cardinals' shortstop Tommy Thevenow hit what should have been a routine double to right field. The ball landed in what New York sportswriters called the "Bloody Angle"—the area between the right field boxes and the wooden bleachers. Ruth, playing right field, couldn't find the ball, although about two-thirds of the spectators at the stadium could. With the ball missing, Thevenow turned his hit into an inside-the-park home run. As the inning ended, Ruth returned to the Yankees' dugout and said, "I kept yellin out there: Where is that stupid ball? Where is that stupid ball? And not a son of a sea cook out there would tell me."[22] Thevenow, who had ranked at the bottom of the list for both clubs during the regular season, would end up the star of the series with a batting average of .417.[23]

The Cardinals' right fielder Southworth hit a home run, breaking the 2–2 tie, and the Cards went on to win the game by a score of 6–2 to even up the series.

The Yankees' loss didn't rattle Colonel Ruppert, who left the stadium smiling and predicting that the Yanks would win the series. Shortly after the game, both teams boarded trains for St. Louis.

En route to St. Louis on the Yankees' train, the Babe, reflecting on his team's loss in the second game, commented to sportswriter Frank Graham, "Still a great pitcher, that Alexander," and added that he "looks as good as he did 10 years ago when he pitched against us in Boston." Outside of some explosive fireworks that were set off by mistake over the Yankees' train as it approached St. Louis, Ruth and the Yankees arrived in St. Louis hardly noticed by anyone.

St. Louis in the 1920s was a booming commercial center. The city had passed an $87 million bond issue for local improvements. Major Albert Bond Lambert, who had operated a balloonist school during World War I, purchased a 170-acre former cornfield, built a triangular landing space in the center and opened it to any aircraft operator free of charge.

As the Cardinals' train approached St. Louis, airplanes flew over it for the last one hundred miles, as the city was preparing to give the players a mid-series reception unheard of in modern times. Business in the downtown area was suspended for two hours, and over ten thousand people jammed the streets for a reception for their pennant-winning Cardinals.

On October 4, 1926, an unprecedented tumultuous mid-series reception was held for the Cardinals in the streets of St. Louis the day before the third game of the World Series: 120 members of the musicians' union led a twenty-five-car motorcade carrying the Cardinals' players as thousands took to the streets to celebrate the first pennant-winning team in St. Louis since 1888. Mayor Miller at times had to use his fists to get through the crowds. *Bettmann/CORBIS.*

The *Christian Science Monitor* described the atmosphere in this way:

> *The flag-bedecked, banner-hung City of St. Louis was entirely all baseball. A celebration that puts in the background all other red letter days in the Mississippi River City's history from the visits of Presidents to Armistice Day is going on incessantly. Cowbells, horns, whistles, electric car gongs, fireworks, decorated automobiles, costumed celebrators all have their places in the greatest season of festivities the city has ever known.*[24]

As the Cardinals' victory train reached the Washington Avenue station on Monday, October 4, pandemonium broke out in the city. Crowds rushed the players, and the most popular of all, Rogers Hornsby, was literally engulfed by people. Women ran their fingers through his hair and tried to kiss him. Men pounced on his shoulders. Mayor Victor Miller, attempting to escort Hornsby, ended up fistfighting his way through the crowd. After being separated from Rogers, his wife and son, Billy, burst into tears.

A podium was set up near the station, where Mayor Miller welcomed the team and presented Rogers Hornsby with a $4,000 Lincoln sedan paid for by St. Louis businessmen. He presented each member of the team with an engraved white gold watch valued at $100 wholesale, as well as a new pair of shoes.

After the presentations, there was a parade through the streets of St. Louis, which was followed by thousands of cheering fans. A platoon of motorcycle policemen led the way, followed by the band from the musicians' union, a six-foot banner of a redbird and nine boys dressed as redbirds, each carrying a bat over his shoulder. Then came the players in a twenty-five-car cavalcade, with three players in each car. As the cavalcade made its way, thousands cheered, ticker tape cascaded from the buildings and fireworks popped on the sidewalks. The motorcade traveled in a sea of red—there were women in red hats and red dresses and men wearing red ties, carrying red pennants and shouting through red megaphones. Grover Cleveland Alexander and his wife Amy rode in one car and the last car brought Rogers Hornsby, his wife Jeannette and son Billy in their brand-new Lincoln. To the amusement of everyone along the parade route, a giant forty-foot banner was unfurled that said, "Rog, Got an Extra Ticket?"

The players were relieved to reach Market Square, where a reviewing stand was set up, and they left to return the next day to resume the series at Sportsman's Park. Martin J. Haley, a baseball writer for the *Globe-Democrat* and a World War I veteran, would describe the receptions as "more impressively enthusiastic than that awarded the noble sons of the Mound City on their victorious return from the World War seven and a half years ago."[25] "Mound City" was a common nickname for St. Louis in 1926, originating from the large number of Native American burial mounds in the city.

Along the parade route a midget on crutches told a reporter, "I ain't got no $25 to pay a scalper for a reserved seat" as he boarded a trolley car, saying he would go out to Sportsman's Park and wait all night for an unreserved seat.[26]

Babe had done so well during the 1926 season that he decided to package his technique and the *St. Louis Post-Dispatch* ran an advertisement that read, "I made my comeback! So can you! Babe Ruth," which implied that just as the Babe had come back from a miserable 1925 season, any person could get into shape and stay fit by purchasing Babe Ruth's Health System. The ad said the health course cost twelve dollars and provided a coupon to send in with one dollar to get started. It gave an address on Broadway in New York City to send the money to.

Sensing the magnitude of the World Series, Dr. George W. Orton, director of athletics at the Sesqui-Centennial Exposition, wired Commissioner of Baseball K.M. Landis inviting the Yankees and the Cardinals to play the seventh game, if needed, at Sesqui-Centennial Stadium in Philadelphia. Dr. Orton pointed out in his telegram that the exposition's stadium had a much larger seating capacity than either Yankee Stadium or Sportsman's Park and that it was in neutral territory.[27]

As Johnny Sylvester's condition worsened, his parents asked if there was anything they could do to make him happy. Weakly, but with a smile, he informed them that he would like a baseball, adding that he'd like it to be one that was used in a World Series game.[28]

Johnny's father, Horace C. Sylvester Jr., was the vice-president of the National City Company of New York, a company affiliated with the National City Bank. Mr. Sylvester approached George D. Buckley, who was the newly appointed vice-president of First National City Bank. Buckley was a large Irishman from Iowa who had played football for the University of Chicago. In 1917, Buckley had been president of Crowell Publishing Co., the company that published several major national magazines including *Collier's*, *American Woman's Home Companion* and *Farm & Fireside*. In 1924, he became the president and publisher of Hearst's *Chicago Herald & Examiner*. Buckley was a giant in the field of publishing in the Midwest and undoubtedly had many connections to professional baseball. "Buck" Buckley was described by Chicago newsmen as "a loud-cursing tough-acting man," but one "who really is mild and human."[29] In 1926, Buckley lived on the Upper East Side of Manhattan in a brownstone with a Kelly green front door.

Mr. Sylvester told Buckley about Johnny's illness, and he informed Buckley that Johnny's only request was for a baseball from the World Series. Buckley was extremely sympathetic to Johnny's serious condition and agreed to do whatever he could to help Horace's son. At that point, both the Yankees and the Cardinals were in St. Louis preparing for the third game of the World Series.

Buckley was confident that he would be able to get a ball and he said, "Horace, we'll not only get the ball, but we'll get it signed by the players."[30] Buckley then sent telegrams to representatives of the Cardinals and the Yankees in St. Louis on Tuesday, October 5, 1926. In the telegrams, he told of Johnny's serious medical condition and relayed Johnny's one dying wish.

Game three took place at Sportsman's Park in St. Louis. Sportsman's Park actually belonged to the St. Louis Browns, whose owner, Phil Ball, had leased it to the Cardinals and in contemplation of the Cardinals' championship games spent over $600,000 to expand the stadium's capacity from eighteen thousand to thirty-three thousand.

But even with the addition, Sportsman's Park was an aging park that couldn't compare to Yankee Stadium. Senators infielder Ossie Bluege described it this way: "You should have been in the old St. Louis ballpark. It was a rat hole, that's what it was. You couldn't leave your shoes or gloves on the floor because rats would come up and chew them up. They had no shower stalls, one pipe in the middle of the room, hot and cold water, but it never got real cold because it was beastly hot in St. Louis."[31]

On Tuesday, October 5, 1926, despite a rain-filled, cold and gray day, an overcapacity crowd of 37,708 spectators filled Sportsman's Park, as multitudes wanted to be present to witness the first World Series game in St. Louis by the Cardinals in the modern era. The rain commenced during batting practice at noon, and finally when the sun came out the band played "It Ain't Gonna Rain No More."

The opposing pitchers were "Dutch" Ruether for the Yankees and Jesse Haines for the Cardinals. Haines overpowered the Yankees, not with his traditional knuckle ball, but with fastballs. As Haines was silencing the Yankees' bats, Huggins brought in Bob Shawkey and Myles Thomas to try to stop the Cardinals' offense. Lou Gehrig managed two hits, but the rest of the Yankees collectively only had three.

In the top of the fourth inning, Ruth singled and was moved to second by Meusel, who tapped a ball back to Haines. Then, in spite of what the band had played, heavy rain began to fall and play was suspended.

The rain delay lasted thirty-two minutes. According to sportswriter Bill Cunningham, during the delay two large policemen went into the dugouts of both teams with shiny new baseballs. "It's for a sick kid," they said, "scratch your names on here, will yuh?"[32]

On the ball signed by the Cardinals there was an inscription: "To Johnny Sylvester: Hoping you will soon by batting 1,000 per cent in good health– The Cards!" It was also autographed by Rogers Hornsby and fourteen other Cardinals' players.

On the ball signed by the Yankees there was an inscription: "To Johnny Sylvester: We're glad to know that you knocked the bug for a homerun–The Yanks!" The ball was autographed by Bob Meusel, Pat Collins, Herb Pennock and Mark Koenig. On another face of the ball Babe Ruth wrote, "I'll knock a homer for you in Wednesday's game," and signed it, "Babe Ruth."

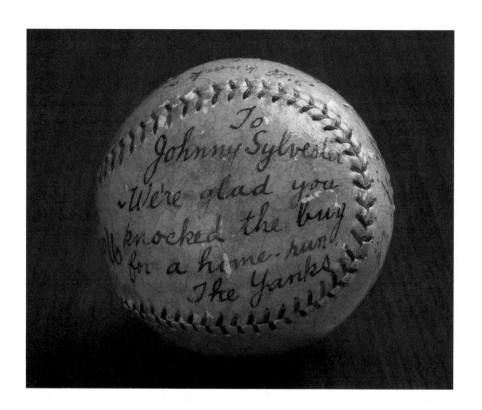

The autographed baseball sent to Johnny Sylvester by the New York Yankees in October of 1926, containing Babe Ruth's special pledge. *Photos by Brett Wood, courtesy of the Babe Ruth Birthplace and Museum and John Dale Sylvester Jr.*

Oct. 4, '26
St. Louis - Chicago via route - 2:30
Time - 19 Hrs. - 15 Min. Flts. - 23

Oct. 5, '26
Chicago - St. Louis via route - 2:50
Time - 22 Hrs 05 Min. Flts - 26

Oct. 6, '26
St. Louis - Chicago via route
2 Hrs. 50 Min.
Time - 24 Hrs - 55 Min. Flts - 29

Oct. 7, '26
Chicago - St. Louis - via route
2 Hrs. 55 Min.
Time - 27 Hrs 50 Min Flts. 32

Oct. 13, '26
St. Louis - Chicago via route - 2 Hrs. 40 M
Time - 30 Hrs. 30 Min. Flts - 35

Oct. 14, '26
Chicago - St. Louis via route - 3 Hrs.
Time - 33 Hrs - 30 Min. Flts - 38

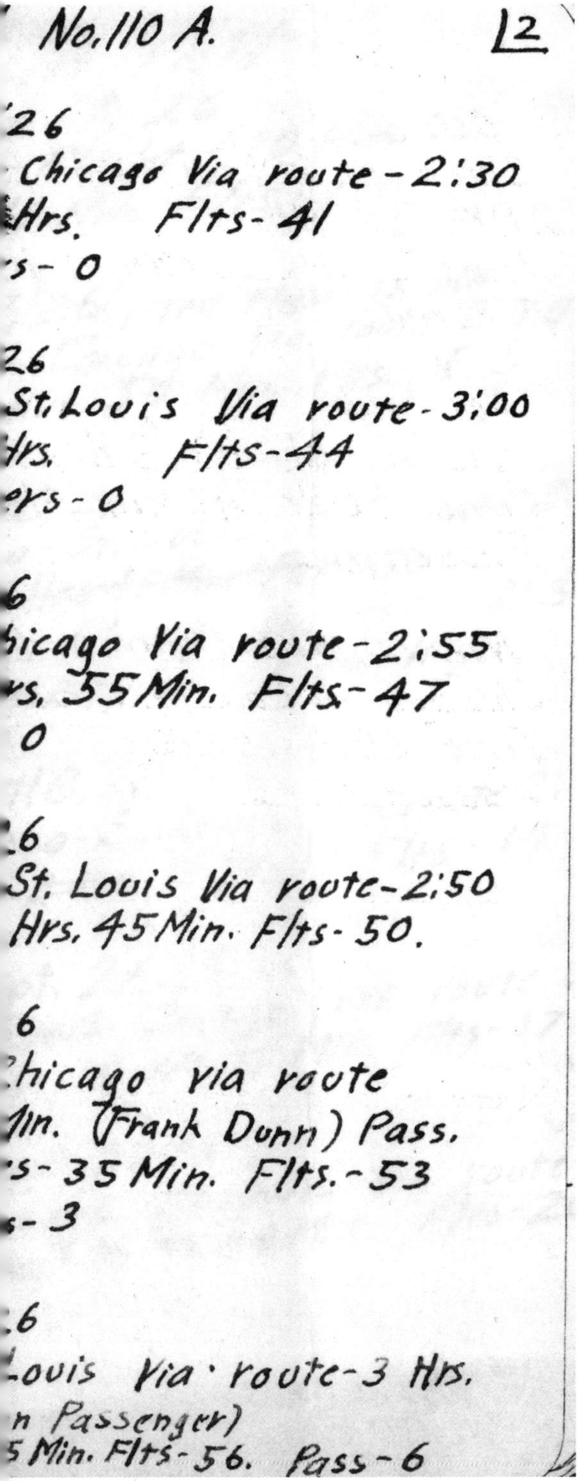

No. 110 A.   L2

'26
Chicago Via route - 2:30
Hrs.   Flts- 41
's - 0

26
St. Louis Via route - 3:00
Hrs.   Flts - 44
ers - 0

6
hicago Via route - 2:55
's, 35 Min. Flts - 47
    0

.6
St. Louis Via route - 2:50
Hrs. 45 Min. Flts - 50.

6
Chicago via route
Min. (Frank Dunn) Pass.
's - 35 Min. Flts. - 53
s - 3

.6
Louis via route - 3 Hrs.
n Passenger)
5 Min. Flts - 56.   Pass - 6

The logbook Charles A. Lindbergh used while he was the chief pilot for the Robertson Aircraft Corporation when he flew the airmail route between St. Louis and Chicago in the fall of 1926. Had the autographed baseballs destined for Johnny Sylvester been delayed by one day, they would have been flown by Lindbergh to Chicago on his flight of October 6, 1926. *Courtesy of Missouri Historical Society.*

As play resumed, Ruth was left stranded on second base. Haines shut out the Yankees, and he himself knocked a two-run homer in the bottom of the fourth inning. The Cardinals went on to beat the Yankees by a score of 4–0. Haines became one of only two pitchers with a shutout and a homer in a World Series game. Bucky Walters would do it in 1940, pitching for the Cincinnati Red Legs. When it was all over, even Grover Cleveland Alexander said it was the best pitched game thus far in the series. [33]

In the Yankees' locker room after the game, there was a sense of doom and gloom. The Yankees' bats had been relatively silent thus far in the series. Ruth, however, burst in and yelled, "Who the hell called them Cards a ball club?" He then told his dejected teammates, "They ain't even half a team. We'll start hittin' tomorrow and go through 'em like Dewey went through Manila Bay."[34] The *St. Louis Post-Dispatch* reported Ruth as saying, "I can't see the Cardinals as a ball club, no matter if they did lick us today," adding that he felt Pittsburgh and Cincinnati were better teams and saying that the Cardinals had been lucky by "getting a lot of flukey hits."[35]

According to *Boston Post* sportswriter Bill Cunningham, Ruth's remarks were picked up by the St. Louis newspapers the next morning, and the incensed Cardinals' fans were set and determined to boo and heckle Ruth at game four at every opportunity.[36] But Ruth had other ideas.

Because of Johnny Sylvester's perilous medical condition, the autographed baseballs were sent via airmail to Johnny's father's office in New York City.

In 1926, the United States Post Office maintained a transcontinental airmail route between San Francisco and New York. Mail would be brought by airplanes on "feeder routes" that connected to the transcontinental route. The feeder route from St. Louis brought mail to Chicago, with stops at Springfield and Peoria, Illinois. The St. Louis to Chicago airmail route had been awarded to the Robertson Aircraft Corporation, which inaugurated its service on April 14, 1926. The chief pilot for the Robertson Aircraft Corporation was twenty-four-year-old Charles A. Lindbergh, who had left the University of Wisconsin in Madison to pursue a career in aviation.

The package containing the two autographed baseballs for Johnny Sylvester was taken to Lambert Field in St. Louis for the 3:30 p.m. airmail flight to Chicago. It appears that the package made the plane on October 5. If the package had missed Robertson's flight on October 5, it would have been on a flight on October 6, when the pilot was Charles A. Lindbergh. According to his own flight logs, Charles A. Lindbergh was the pilot who flew the airmail on the St. Louis to Chicago route on October 6, with a flying time of two hours and fifty minutes.[37] Thus, it appears that Charles A. Lindbergh missed transporting the package that contained the precious

Crowds of baseball fans entering Sportsman's Park in St. Louis to watch the third game of the World Series on October 5, 1926. Although the ballpark's capacity had recently been expanded from eighteen thousand to thirty-three thousand, seats were so scarce that some of St. Louis's millionaires took jobs as ushers just to see the games. *Underwood & Underwood/ CORBIS.*

autographed baseballs for Johnny Sylvester by only one day. It was during the St. Louis to Chicago route that Lindbergh decided to attempt to win Raymond Orteig's $25,000 prize by being the first person to fly nonstop across the Atlantic.

Robertson's airplanes consisted of a fleet of five aging deHavilland biplanes painted silver and maroon with "U.S. Mail" written in bold white letters. The trip was often perilous, and less than three weeks before Johnny's baseballs made the trip, Lindbergh had been forced to parachute from his mail plane when he was running out of fuel in a foggy area near Peoria.

The airmail flight from Lambert Field went to Chicago in time to transfer the mail to the overnight flight to New York that made one stop in Cleveland. The package arrived in New York on the morning of October 6. It was then delivered to the office of Horace Sylvester at the National City Company located on Wall Street. According to the *New York Herald Tribune,*

"There were numerous fans in the office of the National City Company and some of them wanted to see the baseballs at once, but Mr. Sylvester took the package home unopened."[38]

As game four was set to begin in St. Louis on Wednesday, October 6, 1926, word spread through the St. Louis newspapers of the disparaging remarks Ruth had made the day before about the Cardinals' team. An editorial in the *St. Louis Post-Dispatch* ridiculed Ruth's remarks and said the "only excuse for this slander is that it was given out in a dressing room interview while the Bam's Airedales were still hot."[39]

Some 38,825 fans jammed into Sportsman's Park to root for the Cardinals, who now had a 2–1 advantage in the series. In light of the slanderous remarks Ruth had made the day before, they were prepared to heckle and boo him. But as Ruth took fielding practice in left field before the game started, he threw balls to those in the bleachers, and when they asked for autographs he complied. Before the game even started, Ruth began to win the crowd over in what sportswriter Heywood Braun called the "winning of the wild."

Flint Rhem, a twenty-game winner for the Cardinals during the regular season, was their starting pitcher, and Waite Hoyt, "the Merry Mortician," was the starter for the Yankees.

The leadoff batter, Combs, struck out, followed by Koenig, who also struck out. With two outs, Ruth came to bat next and swung at Rhem's first pitch, a high fastball over the center of the plate, sending it high over the right field pavilion near the foul line for a distance of 395 feet.[40] Though neither Johnny Sylvester nor the rest of the baseball-viewing world knew it at the time, at that moment Ruth fulfilled his pledge to Johnny Sylvester. The Bambino's blast was caught by a boy named Henry Bascom, who was waiting in Grand Boulevard, anticipating a Ruthian homer.

No one ever described Ruth hitting a home run better than Leo Durocher, who the following year would be Ruth's teammate. Durocher put it this way:

> He'd twirl that big 48-ounce bat around in little circles up at the plate as if he were cranking it up for the Biggest Home Run Ever Hit—you felt that—and when he'd hit one he would hit it like nobody has hit it before or since. A mile high and a mile out. I can see him now, as I did so many times, just look up, drop the bat and start to trot, the little pitter-patter pigeon-toed, high-bellied trot that seemed to say, I've done it before and I'll do it again, but this one was for you.[41]

Babe Ruth hitting his first home run for Johnny Sylvester in the fourth game of the World Series at Sportsman's Park in St. Louis on October 6, 1926. The Cardinals' catcher was Bob O'Farrell. The ball traveled over the right field pavilion for a distance of 395 feet and was caught by a boy named Henry Bascom, who was eagerly awaiting it. *Bettmann/ CORBIS.*

Ruth crossing the plate after hitting his first home run in the fourth game of the 1926 World Series in Sportsman's Park in St. Louis. The day before, the Babe had predicted, "We'll start hitting tomorrow and go through 'em like Dewey went through Manila Bay." *Bettmann/CORBIS.*

Babe Ruth knocking home run number two for Johnny Sylvester off Clint Rhem in the third inning of the fourth game of the 1926 World Series in Sportsman's Park, St. Louis. This mammoth homer went 515 feet, cleared the right center field pavilion and broke the front window of the Wells Motor Company across the street on Grand Avenue. *Bettmann/CORBIS.*

In the bottom of the first, the Cardinals tied the game when Hornsby singled with two men on base. In the top of the third inning, Combs and Koenig both flied out. Ruth came up for his second at-bat. Again he swung at the first pitch and belted it for another home run. According to the play-by-play announcer, "The home run was much harder than the other one. It went way out, half way between centre and right field, driven almost on a line, just about as hard as any ball Ruth or any one else ever hit."[42] The ball traveled outside of Sportsman's Park and broke a storefront window of the Wells Motor Car Company, located on Grand Avenue. The distance for Ruth's second homer was 515 feet.[43]

The Wells window was five feet by nine feet and was completely shattered, with only a small sliver of glass remaining. The ball did not enter the showroom, but bounced back on the sidewalk and started rolling, where it was snatched up by a young boy. Employees from Wells ran out of the showroom and tried to catch the boy, but he was too fast for them.

The broken window at the Wells Motor Car Company on Grand Avenue in St. Louis that was shattered by Ruth's second home run. After breaking the window, the ball rolled onto the sidewalk, where a young boy retrieved it and outran employees from the company who were after him in hot pursuit. Before leaving St. Louis, Ruth would visit the window and pose for photographs. *Transcendental Graphics*.

According to the *St. Louis Post-Dispatch*, "The window which Ruth smashed has been broken on four other occasions by home runs, but this was the Babe's first offense. The window is insured and each time it is broken the insurance company collects from the ball club."[44]

The score was now 2–1, with Ruth having made both runs. In the fourth inning, the Yankees added another run, as Tony Lazzeri scored when Joe Dugan hit a long fly ball toward center and left and Cardinals' outfielders Chick Hafey and Taylor Douhit collided. In the bottom of the fourth, the Cardinals scored 2 runs and took over the lead by a score of 4–3.

Reinhardt went in to pitch in the fifth inning. The Yankees tied the game when Koenig hit a double and Earle Combs scored. During Ruth's at-bat, he received nothing but bad pitches and walked to first base. The Yankees added another run when Gehrig was walked with bases loaded. The score was now 5–4, Yankees. Herman Bell came in to pitch for Reinhardt. He was known as "Jingle Bell" to distinguish him from the third baseman Lester Bell, who was known as "Tinker Bell."

In the sixth inning on a 3–2 pitch, the Babe walloped the ball and hit his third home run of the day clear into the center field bleachers. The shot traveled more than 530 feet and cleared the 20-foot wall in dead center field. It hopped over the wall and ended up in front of the YMCA building across the street.[45] Some said it was the longest home run ever to be hit in St. Louis. And no one in the history of baseball had ever before hit three home runs in one World Series game. The Yankees were hysterical. Huggins rushed from the dugout to shake Ruth's hand and Lazzeri climbed on top of the Bambino's shoulders. Huggins would say, "I cannot recall when I saw a harder hit ball than his line drive," and added that Ruth "showed himself undisputedly to be the greatest ballplayer that ever entered the game."[46]

This is how Damon Runyon, in his column titled "Just an Accident," described Ruth's home runs on that Wednesday in St. Louis:

> *The crowd thought the first home run by that mighty man, George Herman Babe Ruth, was an accident. The ball was just inside the foul line in right field. They laughed it off with scorn.*
>
> *They felt that the second one, flush, plump into the right field pavilion was intentional, all right, but they continued to laugh not too heartily however.*
>
> *They decided that the third homer, which traveled farther than most folk could carry a baseball in a basket, was rubbing it in, and based entirely on malice.*
>
> *They stopped laughing and began scowling at that mighty man, George Herman Babe Ruth, who suddenly became the soul of affability. Up to*

Babe Ruth arriving at home plate after hitting his third home run in the fourth game of the 1926 World Series at Sportsman's Park, St. Louis. This blast was said to have been the longest home run ever hit in Sportsman's Park. It traveled over 530 feet, clearing the 20-foot wall in center field, bouncing over the wall and ending up across the street in front of the YMCA. All of the home run balls were brought to Ruth after the game and he numbered them #1, #2 and #3. *Bettmann/CORBIS.*

today, that mighty man had been so morose that his friends were a little troubled. They did not suspect he was thinking.

After his third blow, that mighty man smiled all over the place, and also all over his face. He chatted gaily with the boys in the leftfield bleachers in front of which he disports. He as the soul of food humor.[47]

When Ruth took the field after his third homer, the fans in the bleachers gave him a standing ovation. Never mind the slanderous comments he had made the day before about the Cardinals—the Babe had earned the respect of the Cardinals' fans for his magnificent feat.

In the eighth inning, Babe walked on four straight balls. The Babe had clearly succeeded in the "winning of the wild," for the Cardinals' crowd yelled, "Let him hit!" after every ball was called.

Waite Hoyt went the distance for the Yankees, and five Cardinals' pitchers made appearances but couldn't stem the Hugmen, who went on to win by a score of 10–5.

The series was now even. The Babe set six new World Series records that day and received over 580 congratulatory telegrams. As he was getting into his street clothes, it was Ruth's turn to whistle "Bye, Bye Blackbird," and all of the other Yankees joined in. All three of the home run balls were brought to Ruth, and he labeled them #1, #2 and #3.

According to *Boston Post* sports columnist Bill Cunningham, in the sixth inning thirty-eight thousand spectators had seen Ruth kneel down as he batted. Cunningham speculated that Ruth had been praying and that he probably said, "Please help me sock it just once more for that kid."[48] He also speculated that when Ruth was taking practice swings, he was doing the sign of the cross. And then, Cunningham added, "Some of the writers remarked that the Babe seemed a trifle blasé as he circled the paths and ducked into the dugout without so much as lifting his cap. The truth of the matter just might reveal that the Babe didn't show them too much of his face—they might have seen something that looked dangerously like tears. For the Babe's just a kid after all."[49]

What cannot be denied is that Ruth set a new record (Ruth had belted two home runs in game two of the 1923 series and had almost made three when Casey Stengel caught his hit to deep center field), and almost as soon as he made it a legend was born. No one had ever hit three home runs in a World Series game before, and he made them for a sick boy.

That evening in Essex Fells, New Jersey, Horace Sylvester brought home the special package for Johnny. Johnny cut the string himself, and according to Johnny's mother, when the baseballs were unwrapped, her son's temperature immediately dropped by two degrees.[50]

Johnny then asked his father if Ruth had hit a home run. His father showed Johnny a newspaper with the headlines of Ruth's three home runs.

Reports of Johnny getting the autographed baseballs appeared in the *New York Times*, the *Newark Evening News*, the *Newark Star Eagle*, the *Caldwell Progress* and every major newspaper in New York City. The Associated Press spread the story to hundreds of newspapers all across the country and to England and France as well.

The next day a very appreciative Horace Sylvester wrote thank-you notes to the managers of both World Series teams. In his letter to Rogers Hornsby he wrote:

Many thanks for the baseball carrying the autographs of yourself and members of the Cardinal team. It was handed to my ailing son by an air mail man and your kindly thought to buoy up the youngster that he is now well out of the woods. The request for the ball came at a time when you had plenty on your mind and its arrival is doubly appreciated![51]

Johnny's father wrote the following to Yankees' manager Miller Huggins:

Your interest in having the Yankee players autograph a baseball for my eleven-year old son, John Dale Sylvester, is highly appreciated. The trophy arrived from St. Louis by air mail and had the instant effect of rallying the spirit of the ailing youngster.

I realize what it meant to you to break into the tussle and excitement of a world's series to get the signatures and I want to assure you that it has brought about all that we anticipated in putting the baseball-loving boy back in the race to regain his health.[52]

Johnny's hometown newspaper, the *Caldwell Progress*, sent a reporter to see him on October 7. The reporter stated that Johnny was bright and cheery and said that when he got well Johnny said he would bring his friends over to try out the new Kiwanis Oval located just behind the *Progress*'s offices.[53]

Over forty-one thousand people, the largest crowd to attend the games in St. Louis, crammed Sportsman's Park on Thursday, October 7, 1926, for the fifth game of the series. The two starting left-handed pitchers from game one faced each other again—Herb Pennock, "the Knight of Kennett Square," and "Wee" Willie Sherdel for the Cards—both on four days' rest.

Game five went scoreless until the bottom of the fourth, when the Cards scored the first run with a double by Jim Bottomley, followed by a single by Lester Bell.

Johnny Sylvester had been told to rest that day, but he awakened right after the Cardinals took the lead in the fourth. He immediately asked, "Did Babe Ruth hit another homer?" A reporter for the *Evening World* took the play-by-play up to him between innings. When he was told of Bottomley's run, Johnny said, "That one run doesn't matter. The Yanks are going to win. I just know Babe Ruth will win the game."

In the top of the sixth, the bespectacled Cardinals' outfielder Chick Hafey misjudged a routine fly by leadoff batter Herb Pennock, running in when he should have run out, and he slipped and fell and turned what should have been an easy out into a double. Mark Koenig then singled, evening the score at 1–1. After hearing that the Yanks had tied the score, Johnny hollered for his supper, which prompted his nurse to say, "It's a good sign when they begin to want to eat!" As Johnny hugged his precious autographed baseballs, he said, "Gee, won't I have something to show the kids."

In the bottom of the seventh, the Cards again took the lead when Lester Bell doubled and Bob O'Farrell, the Cards' catcher, singled.

Sherdel continued to pitch a masterful game and skillfully pitched to Ruth—giving him only slow inside pitches—so Ruth went hitless.

In the ninth inning there was another miscue by the Cardinals' fielders, this time by Tommy Thevenow, when Lou Gehrig hit a ball into shallow left. But as Thevenow raced out for it, the wind blew it in and Gehrig raced to second for a double. Tony Lazzeri then laid down a bunt, bringing Gehrig to third. As Joe Dugan, "the pride of Scarsdale," approached the batting cage, he was called back by Miller Huggins, who put up pinch hitter Ben Pashcal. Pashcal's single tied the game.

Herb Pennock held the Cardinals scoreless in the bottom of the ninth and the game went into the top of the tenth all tied at 2–2. Leading off the tenth, Mark Koenig singled. Sherdel pitched to Ruth but walked him. Bob Meusel then made a sacrifice bunt, advancing Koenig and Ruth.

Lazzeri hit a long sacrifice fly in the tenth, which enabled Koenig to score for the go-ahead run. Pennock shut out the Cardinals in the bottom of the tenth, and the Yankees won the game 3–2; they now led the series by the same margin. The win for Herb Pennock was his fourth victory without a defeat in World Series games.

The Yanks needed to win only one more game at Yankee Stadium to win the series, and they would have the home field advantage. The *New York Times*'s James R. Harrison pointed out that not since 1907 had the visiting team taken the seventh game of the World Series. Cards' player-manager Rogers Hornsby had other thoughts, however, saying, "We play best in enemy territory."

As the forty-one thousand spectators left the game, it was tough to find any of the 506 taxicabs that were supposed to be operating that day in the city of St. Louis.

A reporter from the *Evening World* told the recovering boy, "Johnny, you don't look as though you had been sick; you look as though one of the kids at school had given you a shiner." To which Johnny replied, "If I'd gotten this eye that way, you can bet there'd be some kid who would get one like it when I get back to school." The nurse said that the doctors were discontinuing treatments and were prescribing for him little more than good food, sunshine and rest.

On October 8, 2006, football great "Red" Grange, "the Galloping Ghost" and "Phantom of the Prairies," hopped on the Johnny Sylvester recovery bandwagon by sending him a personal letter and an autographed football. In his letter, Grange promised to score a touchdown for him when he played the first game of the season at Yankee Stadium. "The best of luck to you, Johnny, and hurry up and get into action with the rest of us athletes," wrote Grange.[54]

Red Grange, born Harold Edward Grange in Forksville, Sullivan County, Pennsylvania, on June 13, 1903, was taken by his lumberjack father to live in Wheaton, Illinois, after the death of his mother. It was on the University of Illinois's football squad that Grange made his reputation. In a game held at a new stadium before a crowd of sixty thousand patrons, he scored four touchdowns, took a break—stating he "needed a breather"—and then returned to the game to score his fifth.

Like Ruth, the press followed Red's every mood. He became a professional on November 22, 1925, signing with the Chicago Bears, and representing him was C.C. "Cash and Carry" Pyle. When Pyle couldn't get the Bears to meet his demands, he had Grange form his own team, the New York Yankees of the American Football League. This team lasted only one season before it merged into the National Football League.

During Red's professional tour, Ruth wanted to meet Grange, and one night invited himself up to Red's hotel room. As the story goes, the Babe's advice for Grange was, "Kid, don't believe anything they write about you, and don't pick up too many dinner checks."[55]

As McNamee and Carlin took to the radio airwaves for game six from Yankee Stadium in the Bronx, there was one person who would not be listening in. Johnny Sylvester's physician decided that the additional excitement would not be good for the boy who on Wednesday had started on his road to recovery with the arrival of the autographed baseballs. Johnny's parents knew that he could not sleep if the game were on, so they told him the game had been postponed. "You're sure?" he asked. According to reports, Johnny then fell asleep in minutes, with his parents thinking of repeating the same procedure the following day.[56]

On October 9, Babe Ruth acknowledged this about his home runs from game four:

> *I get lots of requests for autographed baseballs from sick boys but this kid asked for a home run. Wednesday I got hold of the first one and it went into the bleachers. "There's one for the sick kid," I said to myself.*

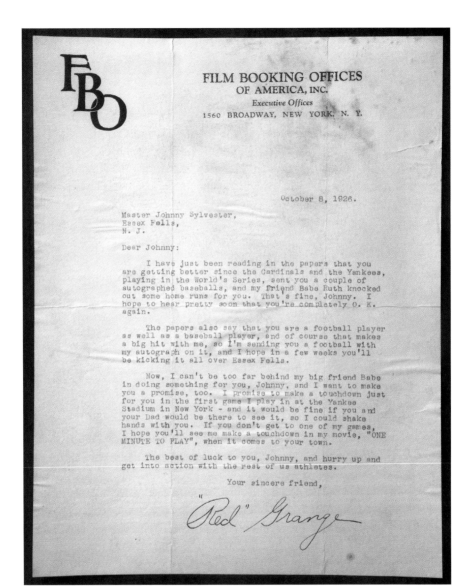

FILM BOOKING OFFICES
OF AMERICA, INC.
Executive Offices
1560 BROADWAY, NEW YORK, N. Y.

October 8, 1926.

Master Johnny Sylvester,
Essex Fells,
N. J.

Dear Johnny:

I have just been reading in the papers that you are getting better since the Cardinals and the Yankees, playing in the World's Series, sent you a couple of autographed baseballs, and my friend Babe Ruth knocked out some home runs for you. That's fine, Johnny. I hope to hear pretty soon that you're completely O. K. again.

The papers also say that you are a football player as well as a baseball player, and of course that makes a big hit with me, so I'm sending you a football with my autograph on it, and I hope in a few weeks you'll be kicking it all over Essex Fells.

Now, I can't be too far behind my big friend Babe in doing something for you, Johnny, and I want to make you a promise, too. I promise to make a touchdown just for you in the first game I play in at the Yankee Stadium in New York - and it would be fine if you and your Dad would be there to see it, so I could shake hands with you. If you don't get to one of my games, I hope you'll see me make a touchdown in my movie, "ONE MINUTE TO PLAY", when it comes to your town.

The best of luck to you, Johnny, and hurry up and get into action with the rest of us athletes.

Your sincere friend,

"Red" Grange

Letter from Red Grange to Johnny Sylvester telling him he had read that Johnny was a football player as well as a baseball player, and that he was sending him an autographed football and hoping that in a few weeks he would be "kicking it all over Essex Fells." Young Johnny did exactly that and played with the football for many years, in the process erasing the autograph of the famous football star. *Johnny Sylvester Scrapbook.*

Autographed football given to Johnny Sylvester by football star Red Grange in 1926.
Courtesy of John Dale Sylvester Jr.

Perhaps it sounds foolish, but the next time I came up I said to myself, "Maybe you can make another for the kid" and I socked one over the fence. By that time I kind of got the notion the kid was pulling for me. Then I made No. 3. Say, if I'd had a chance I believe I could have made another, but they passed me.[57]

Ruth's comments came in a front-page article in the *Boston Herald* with the headline "Babe Ruth's 3 Homers Inspired by Sick Lad's Request, He Says," and similar headlines appeared in papers all over the country through the Associated Press.

In a letter dated October 9, 1926, written to Johnny Sylvester by Babe Ruth before the start of game six, Ruth tells Johnny that he hadn't forgotten about him and apologized for not having visited him. In the letter, Ruth states that he "will try and knock you another homer maybe two today."[58]

Rogers Hornsby also wrote a letter to Johnny on October 9, saying that if "Babe Ruth is going to hit a home run for you I only hope I can hit two for you."

In game six, Yankee Skipper Miller Higgins chose "Sailor Bob" Shawkey, a right-hander, to face the winner of game two, Grover Cleveland Alexander. Shawkey had received his nautical nickname from serving in the navy

Handwritten letter from Babe Ruth to Johnny Sylvester mistakenly dated October 9, 1923, in which Ruth promises to try and knock "another homer maybe two" in the sixth game of the 1926 World Series against the St. Louis Cardinals. Ruth did not hit a homer in the sixth game, but made his fourth series homer in the seventh game at Yankee Stadium on October 10, 1926. *Johnny Sylvester Scrapbook.*

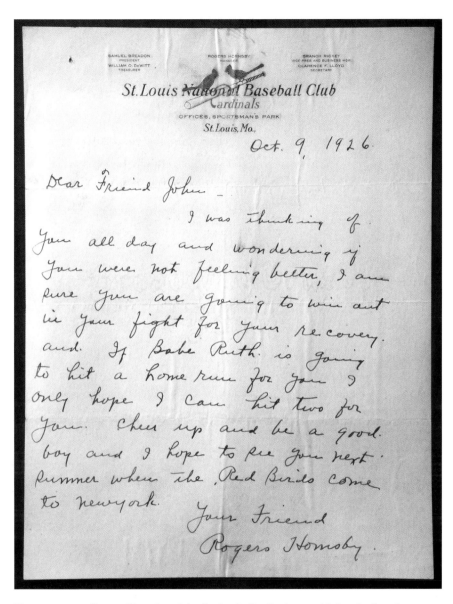

Player-manager Rogers Hornsby of the St. Louis Cardinals sent this handwritten letter to Johnny Sylvester dated October 9, 1926, saying that if Babe Ruth is going to hit a home run for him "I only hope I can hit two for you." Hornsby had previously signed the baseball that the Cardinals had sent. *Johnny Sylvester Scrapbook.*

during World War I. The *Chicago Daily Tribune* headlined the game by saying, "Cards Pin Hope on Ex-Bargain Counter Pickup."[59] After returning from the Great War to the Major Leagues in 1919, Shawkey had been a 20-game winner and repeated it in 1920 and 1922. But in 1926, Shawkey's regular season record was a modest 8–6.

In the Cardinals' locker room before the game, Rogers Hornsby exhorted his team, "If we don't do it today, there aren't any more series but, there is going to be more series. We've got to win today and we've got to win tomorrow. So, get out there, fight your heads off; knock the ball down the pitcher's throat, and don't concede a thing."[60]

The Cards put the game away in the third inning, scoring three runs. Les Bell was the hitting star with a homer, two singles and four RBIs. Billy Southworth scored three times, and the Rajah drove in three runs.

The Cardinals went on to win the game by a score of 10–2. At age thirty-nine, Grover Cleveland Alexander became the oldest pitcher in World Series history to pitch a complete game.

In the words of sportswriter Richard Vidmer, "The sluggist Yanks were outslugged, outpitched, outfielded and outplayed about as badly as any championship team can be by another."[61]

And as a good luck omen for the Cardinals, earlier in the day in the first race at Fairmount Park Racetrack in Collinsville, Illinois, a black colt named Hornsby won his maiden race, paying his supporters $8.90 for a straight ticket. It was reported that many St. Louisans cashed in heavily on the race.

For the third successive year, the World Series would go to the seventh game. This would, however, be only the fifth time a seventh game was played since the World Series started in 1903. The World Series had always been the best of seven, except for the first one in 1903 and for four seasons from 1919 through 1922.

As the Cardinals' players woke up on Sunday morning, October 10, 1926, in their rooms at the Alamac Hotel at Broadway and Seventy-first Street, they were convinced that the weather was too bad to play in. They were taken by surprise when Commissioner Mountain Landis called and said, "It's on boys, get your asses ready to play."

A combination of decreased interest in attending seventh games and rumors that the game was going to be postponed on account of rain brought out only approximately thirty-eight thousand fans to Yankee Stadium for what was certainly the most important game to be played at the stadium up until that date. But there was plenty of excitement in the air. In the words of Rogers Hornsby, "The very air tingled. You couldn't step on that field without experiencing a feeling that this whole setup was a grand, grand thing."

Babe Ruth crossing home plate after hitting his fourth world series home run in the third inning of the seventh game of the 1926 World Series at Yankee Stadium in the Bronx, New York. In the foreground is Cardinals' catcher Bob O'Farrell. The Yanks lost the game 3–2 and the series to the St. Louis Cardinals. *Bettman/CORBIS.*

Jesse Haines, who had shut the Yankees out in St. Louis in game three, was the starting pitcher for the Cardinals, and Waite Hoyt, whose regular season record was 16-2, was the starter for the Yankees.

In the third inning with one on base, Ruth hit a 390-foot drive into the right center field bleachers—it was his fourth home run of the series.[62] The Yankees, with Ruth leading the way, were now leading 1–0. But then the Yankees' defense went to pieces. Meusel muffed a fly, another hit went between Meusel and Koenig and Koenig muffed a grounder. The Yankees picked up a second run in the bottom of the sixth on a double by Severeid. The score was now 3–2.

In the bottom of the seventh, Haines walked Earle Combs and Mark Koenig sacrificed him to second. Then the Babe, who had hit a home run in his previous at-bat, was up. Hornsby told Jesse to intentionally walk him. Meusel forced Ruth at second, and Combs went to third. Haines then walked Lou Gehrig, and the bases were loaded with two outs. Haines then wiggled his hand to Hornsby. Hornsby came out to the mound and saw that Jesse, who often threw a knuckle ball, had completely worn the skin off his index finger. Some reports state that his finger was actually bleeding. He had to come out. Hornsby had Sherdel and Rhem warming up in the bullpen.

Everyone in the stadium stared at the left field bleachers in which the Cardinals' bullpen was tucked away to see through the misty haze who would emerge. What they saw was a gangly stoop-shouldered old man wearing a bright red sweater. As he crossed the field, it appeared he had an air of indifference and his small cap was cocked to one side. As the figure came closer to the mound, the fans recognized it as the old Yankee killer from games two and six—Ol' Pete Alexander. As he slowly made his way to the mound with his head down, many thought he was looking at the grass in order to find a four-leafclover. Others thought that he was recovering from drinking either the night before or perhaps having hit his gin in the bullpen. Hornsby would later add to the wild speculation when he said, "Hell, I'd rather have him pitch a crucial game for me drunk than anyone I've ever known sober."[63] With the stage set for one of the defining moments in the World Series, young Tony Lazzeri waited patiently at the plate. A Yankee was on every base. A single would bring in the tying run; a double or better would give the Yankees the lead.

As Alexander approached the mound, Hornsby was out of the Cardinals' dugout. According to Babe Ruth, Hornsby greeted Alexander in the shallow outfield. Others said he went far out into the outfield, and some recalled that he simply went out to the mound. But all accounts state that when Hornsby came up to Alexander, he immediately looked into Ol' Pete's eyes. They appeared clear, so Hornsby was convinced that Alexander had not been drinking in the bullpen and wasn't affected from a celebration the night before. Reports had circulated that Alexander had spent the night after his game six victory celebrating at Billy LaHiff's Speakeasy located at 158 West Forty-eighth Street in Manhattan. Damon Runyon would even spread the story that Hornsby had to send for Alexander from Billy LaHiff's during the game. He clued Alexander in by telling him, "Well, the bases are full, Lazzeri's up and there ain't no place to put him." Alex responded by saying, "Yeah, well, guess I'll have to take care of him then."[64] Alexander then threw three warm-up pitches. But he was in no hurry. Alexander, the wily veteran, knew that the rookie Lazzeri would be getting increasingly more anxious and nervous as time elapsed. The first pitch was wide for a ball. The next pitch was a strike. The next pitch Lazzeri belted deep into the left field stands, and the Yankees were all on the top steps of the dugout ready to meet Lazzeri at home plate, but then the ball, aided by the wind, ended up foul. According to Hornsby, it was foul by about ten inches. Others said it was foul by many feet. On the next pitch, Lazzeri took a strong swing, but he clearly missed Ol' Pete's wicked curve, ending up in an awkward position that was captured by photographers. The inning was over; the Cards were hanging on by a thread and the pitching of a thirty-nine-year-old.

Alexander didn't allow a Yankee batter on base in the eighth inning, and the game entered the bottom of the ninth with the score still 3–2 in favor of the Cardinals.

Ol' Pete got Combs and Koenig out in order in the ninth. With two outs in the bottom of the ninth, the Babe came to bat. This was the dramatic showdown that the fans had come to see—the Bambino facing the crafty Grover Cleveland Alexander. Hornsby walked out to the mound to have a chat with Alexander. Speculation was that Hornsby didn't want Alexander to walk Ruth intentionally. Waiting to bat after Ruth were Meusel and Gehrig. Alexander worked cautiously with Ruth, tailoring every pitch. Alexander pitched a strike and then a ball. Then Ruth fouled one. The crowd went wild. A man listening on the radio in Wilmington, Delaware, while Ruth was at bat dropped dead from a heart attack. Ball two was called, and the excitement mounted. Ol' Pete pitched another ball and the crowd began to boo him. The count was now 3–2. Alexander threw a curve that just missed the plate. Umpire George Hildebrand called ball four. Ruth got his twelfth walk of the series. Ol' Pete thought it was a strike, and he hollered at Hildebrand, "What's wrong with it, anyway?" Hildebrand replied that it had missed the plate by four to five inches. Alexander replied, "For that you might have given an old sonofagun like me a break!"[65] Millions across the country were glued to their radio sets.

The New York Yankees' Anthony "Poosh 'Em Up" Lazzeri striking out in the seventh inning
of the seventh game of the 1926 World Series with two outs and bases loaded. Behind
him is Cardinals' catcher Bob O'Farrell holding onto the pitch from the Cardinals' Grover

Cleveland Alexander. Lazzeri had previously hit Alexander's third pitch deep into the left field stands. Ol' Pete would later say, "If it had stayed fair Tony would have been the hero and I would have been the goat." *National Baseball Hall of Fame Library, Cooperstown, New York.*

Attempting to steal second base, Babe Ruth was tagged out on a throw from Cardinals' catcher Bob O'Farrell to second baseman Rogers Hornsby to end the seventh game of the 1926 World Series. Ruth is the only player to end a World Series by being tagged out on an attempted steal. Years later, Hornsby would say, "My biggest thrill in baseball was making a simple tag on a runner trying to steal second base." *National Baseball Hall of Fame Library, Cooperstown, New York.*

With the Babe on first base, Bob Meusel came up to bat. Lou Gehrig was swinging a bat in the on-deck circle. Alexander didn't want to face Gehrig, and he knew Meusel often fizzled under pressure.[66] It looked like the Yankees had a real shot of winning the game and the series. Meusel had hit .320 during the regular season and was capable of hitting the ball out of the stadium. Alexander came in with a low curve to Meusel and then it happened. The Babe attempted to steal second, and a sharp throw went from catcher Bob O'Farrell to Rogers Hornsby, who tagged out the Babe to end the game and the series. Ed Barrow, the Yankees' business manager, would tell Ruth that it was the only dumb play Ruth ever made in baseball. But Babe, although admitting it was a "rash move," would justify it by saying that he wanted to move the tying run to second base and he was hoping to catch O'Farrell off guard. Ruth was the slowest runner on the Yankees.

Years later, after a remarkable career in baseball, Rogers Hornsby would say, "My biggest thrill in baseball was making a simple tag on a runner trying to steal second base."[67] In the history of baseball, no other player but Ruth has ever been caught stealing to end a World Series.[68]

Radio announcer Graham McNamee would end the seven-game broadcasts stating, "This World Series of 1926—we will never say it again—is over. It has come to a close, and the championship goes west, southwest, down to the sovereign State of Missouri."[69]

While the Cardinals celebrated in their locker room, hailing the Great Alexander as their savior, the Yankees were despondent in theirs because, in the words of Ruth, "what made us feel so badly was that we realized we had licked ourselves."[70]

It was the Babe who conveyed what was the most telling about the loss for the Yankees: "Everybody knew about the celebration old Aleck had attended that Saturday night, figuring he wouldn't be used again for the remainder of the Series. But not many knew that some of our own fellows had been out that same night—prematurely celebrating a Series victory that never came to us."[71]

But Leigh Montville in his splendid biography of Ruth entitled *The Big Bam* found one overriding story:

> *The enduring Big Bam story from the World Series thus was not the attempted steal of second. It wasn't even the three-home-run game or the four home runs in the Series or the .300 batting average or even the ten records he set. It was the story of Johnny Sylvester, the 11-year-old boy from Essex Fells (sic), New Jersey, pulled from death's grasp at the last moment by the heroics of a big lug half a continent away. Fact and myth and good PR, the new science, merged with marketing and America's great love for pathos to create perfection. Johnny Sylvester and the Babe. This was the best story of all.[72]*

Chapter Three

Oh boy I'm lucky
Oh, say I'm lucky
This is my lucky day!
–Music by Ray Henderson
Words by B.G. DeSylva and Lew Brown (1926)

Things were rather dark for Johnny Sylvester on Monday morning, October 11, reported the *New York World*.[73] The World Series had ended and Johnny could hear his school chums knock a baseball around the adjoining lot and another group passing a football. He was tired of being confined to bed and worried about how much schoolwork he would have to make up from his long absence.

That same day, St. Louis had a mammoth celebration for the triumphant Cardinals in the streets of St. Louis. Rogers Hornsby, however, parted with his team and traveled to Austin, Texas, for the belated funeral of his mother.

As the Cardinals were being fêted at a giant celebration of over one million people, Babe Ruth motored nineteen miles due west of New York City to Essex Fells, New Jersey, to visit one person: a recovering Johnny Sylvester.

Accompanying Ruth were his manager and a reporter named Elenore Kellogg from the *New York Daily News*. The manager undoubtedly was Christy Walsh, although none of the newspaper accounts would disclose that he was with Ruth for the visit. His presence would make sense, since Walsh had coordinated all the barnstorming games, one of which Ruth would play later that same day. According to Kellogg, the trip was arranged by the *Daily News*.[74] Ruth was set to play in a barnstorming game in Bradley Beach, New Jersey, that day, but the visit to the boy he dedicated his World Series home runs to would come first. Instead of taking the train to Bradley Beach as planned, he went by roadster to Essex Fells.

Cardinals on October 11, 1926, following their World Series victory over New York Yankees. Chamber of Commerce estimated more than a million baseball celebrants participated in the memorable celebration.

Donated by Mrs. Rachel Breadon, 1953.

The welcome home reception for the St. Louis Cardinals on October 11, 1926, following their World Series victory over the New York Yankees. The St. Louis Chamber of Commerce estimated more than a million baseball fans participated in the celebration. Unfortunately, the celebration would be marred by the death of two people and over thirty injured. *National Baseball Hall of Fame Library, Coooperstown, New York.*

Babe rang the front door of the Sylvesters' two-story colonial house located in the center of the small borough. The Sylvesters' maid opened the door. Johnny, hearing the bell, thought it was probably just another doctor who had come to examine him. "I'm here to see Johnny," said a large, tall man in a camel coat. "Who are you?" asked the maid. "I'm Babe Ruth." Surprisingly, the maid had no idea who Babe Ruth was, and she went and asked Johnny's nurse. "Two gentlemen to see Mr. Johnny." She went upstairs and told Johnny and his mother that there was a man named Babe Ruth downstairs who wanted to see Johnny. She was then instructed to show Ruth up to the second-floor bedroom where Johnny was recovering.

Johnny's six-year-old sister Ruth was standing by the doorway, and she never forgot the vision of Babe Ruth ducking his head in order to enter Johnny's room.[75] Johnny himself would recall that Ruth "filled up the whole doorway."[76] Ruth stood at the doorway for a while watching Johnny's eyes widen. He then went into Johnny's room and introduced his manager and Miss Elenore Kellogg, the reporter from the *Daily News*, to Johnny, his mother and his nurse, Miss Oriell. Then there was a search to find the finest and strongest chairs in the Sylvester household for the distinguished guests. Besides Ruth, Johnny's brother Horace III, three years older, was also standing nearby.

Paul Gallico, the sports editor for the *New York Daily News*, would give his classic version of Ruth's entrance to Johnny's room: "The door opened and it was God himself who walked into the room, straight from his glittering throne. God dressed in a camel's hair polo coat and a flat, camel hair's cap. God with a flat nose and little piggy eyes, a big grin and a fat black cigar sticking out of the side of it."[77]

Ruth approached the bed and took Johnny's small, pale hand in his large one. Johnny was tongue-tied and could only grin. "Hello Johnny," said the Babe. Johnny could only say, "My gosh." According to Elenore Kellogg, who was present, "Over the child's pale face spread a look of such ecstasy that Babe himself was somewhat at a loss for words."[78] "Glad to meet you," said the Babe, "how do you feel?" "Fine," replied Johnny. Ruth presented Johnny with a baseball, on which was written, "The last ball used in the first game of the World Series. Yankees 2, Cardinals 1." Under each of the teams' names were the pitchers' names: Pennock and Sherdel.

The *New York Times* reported that when Johnny's sister—who sported a short haircut—came into the room, Babe said, "Nice looking brother you have there."[79] Ruth Sylvester never remembered that part.[80] Johnny finally told the Babe, "I'm sorry the Yanks lost the series."

A telephone call came in for Babe and he told Johnny that he had to go, as he had another engagement that he was two hours late for, but he would

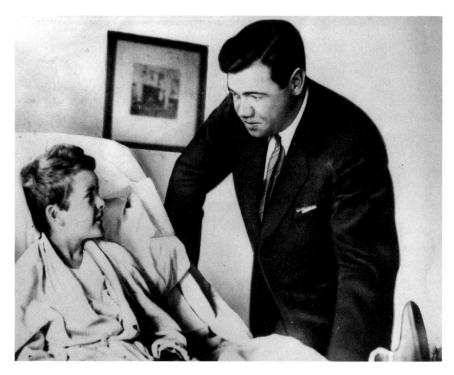

Babe Ruth with eleven-year-old Johnny Sylvester at his bedside in his room at his home in Essex Fells, New Jersey, on October 11, 1926. Johnny Sylvester's sister Ruth would always remember the Babe ducking his head as he entered the room. Eyewitness reporter Elenore Kellogg of the *New York Daily News* wrote that "over the child's pale face spread a look of such ecstasy that Babe himself was somewhat at a loss for words." *The New York Daily News.*

come back soon. "Goodbye Johnny," said Ruth. "Goodbye Babe," said Johnny. The visit had lasted for nearly half an hour.

After Ruth left, Johnny said, "Ain't he big," and hugged his baseballs, as well as the football Red Grange had given him.[81] He told his mother that he had a million things to ask the Babe, but he couldn't get them out. It was reported that he hummed to the song "This Is My Lucky Day" being played on the radio. He vowed to establish a museum in his Essex Fells home for all his cherished sports memorabilia.

The next day the *Newark Star-Eagle* reported, "As a result of the Babe's visit the history of Essex Fells promises to become divided in two parts— before the coming of Ruth, and after. It was forecast today that in years to come old-timers would speak about 'the time when Babe Ruth came to see Johnny Sylvester.'"[82]

After leaving Johnny's house, Babe, Walsh and Kellogg headed to Bradley Beach at the Jersey Shore by motorcar for a game between the Babe

Ruth All Stars and the Brooklyn Royal Colored Giants. Mayor Frank C. Borden Jr., City Commissioner Bernard V. Poland and Robert Lowenstein, along with hundreds of other citizens of Bradley Beach, had organized a welcoming reception and parade for the Babe, who was to arrive on the 11:06 a.m. train from New York. The welcoming party waited at the station, and when the Babe didn't get off the train as expected, they were shocked. The reception was breaking up when the group learned that Ruth had gone first to Essex Fells and was motoring down.

When Ruth, Walsh and Kellogg reached Eatontown, they were escorted by two motorcycle policemen into Bradley Beach. Upon Ruth's arrival at about 2:00 p.m., Mayor Frank C. Borden said Ruth was late for a good cause. Ruth told the crowds, "Johnny's a fine looking boy. I'm glad I went to see him. He's coming along fine. He's going to get well."[83] And then, reported the *Newark Evening News*, "The Bambino, a better physician than hundreds with their shingles out, went on to play ball."[84] Ruth was presented with a pair of pajamas and a radio set.

As Ruth entered the ballpark, he was wildly acclaimed by more than five hundred small boys. They swarmed around him, making it difficult for him to reach the players' bench.

Ruth hit two balls over the fence during the game, which, according to the rules, counted as doubles. Over five thousand spectators saw Babe's team lose 3–1 to the Brooklyn Royal Colored Giants. It was quite typical of the barnstorming teams to have games with teams from the African American leagues. Babe's manager, Christy Walsh, would have been the one to book the opposing team.

The Brooklyn Royal Colored Giants were part of the Eastern Colored League in 1926, and the team was owned by a white entrepreneur named Nathaniel Calvin Strong. Nat Strong owned two automobiles: a seven-passenger Pierce Arrow and a Cadillac that the team used in its travels. During his career, Strong booked many games for baseball clubs throughout the East and later pioneered night baseball.

The day after Ruth's surprise visit, Johnny's health continued to improve and he held forth a mini-press conference in his room with some of his friends and a syndicated reporter. Johnny was quoted as saying he was "already counting the days until he can get up." And he had dreamed the night before that he had been playing baseball with the Bambino.[85]

The next day, Babe's visit to Johnny in Essex Fells made the front page of the *New York Times*, the *New York Daily News*, the *Boston Post* and a score of other newspapers across the country. The *Times*'s headline read, "'Dr'. Babe Calls on his Boy Patient."

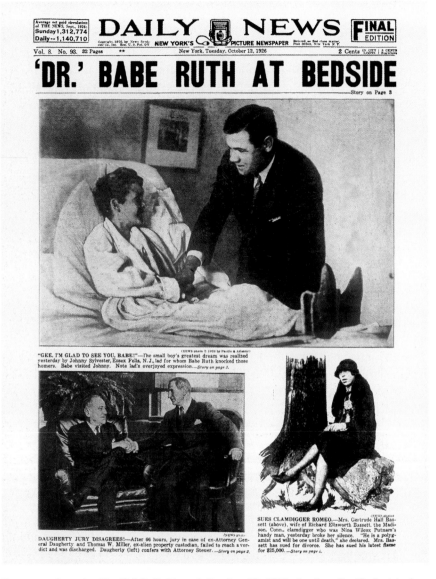

Front page from the *New York Daily News* of October 12, 1926, the day after Ruth visited Johnny in Essex Fells, New Jersey. The visit would also make front-page headlines in the *New York Times* and the *Boston Post*. New York Daily News.

On October 12, 1926, Johnny Sylvester became the most famous eleven-year-old boy in America. An advertisement for copies of the *Democrat Chronicle* and *Rochester Herald* of October 12, 1926, featured Babe Ruth's trip to Johnny Sylvester's home in Essex Fells, New Jersey. *Johnny Sylvester Scrapbook.*

The story spread to newspapers throughout the country. On October 18, 1926, *Time* magazine reported the visit. But the story of the visit, like many other versions, was inaccurate. *Time* reported that Johnny "was dying of blood poisoning in Essex Fields, N.J."[86] But what was true was that Johnny Sylvester had become the most famous eleven-year-old boy in America.

The story was depicted by cartoonists as well. Cartoonist Harry W. Haenigsen saw humor in the idea of sports celebrities sending trophies to help cure sick boys. Haenigsen was born in New York City in 1900, and after studying engineering he enrolled in the Arts Student League in New York and was a cartoonist and illustrator for more than sixty years. He began as an illustrator and columnist for the *New York Evening World* in 1919. He would later cover the Lindbergh kidnapping trial for the *New York Herald Tribune* and be the creator of such popular comic strips as *Simeon Batts*, *Our Bill* and *Penny*.

A few days after the Babe's visit, Johnny received through the mail, without any public fanfare or publicity, an autographed baseball signed by Lou Gehrig. With it was a note in which Gehrig explained that the enclosed baseball had made the last out in the World Series and although he had been saving it, he thought that Johnny might like it instead. According to Jack Cavanagh, "The ball that struck out Lazzeri stayed in the game for two more innings and no one knows where it went."[87] Quite possibly it ended up with an eleven-year-old boy in Essex Fells, New Jersey. In remembering Gehrig's kind gesture years later, Johnny would comment, "I guess everything you read about his quiet elegance is true."[88]

The year 1926 was the last of Ruth's three-year contract with the Yankees for a salary of $52,000 per year. The big question the public had was what he would seek now. The speculation in the press on October 11 was that he would seek the unheard of salary of $150,000 per year.[89] It was estimated that Ruth's presence at Yankee Stadium brought in an additional $500,000 of revenue yearly and that he was earning more than $3,000 at each of his barnstorming games.[90] In 1926, Ruth's total income—between his salary, his barnstorming and his vaudeville tour—exceeded $250,000. In the end, Ruth would end up with a salary of $70,000 for the 1927 season.

Leaving Bradley Beach, Babe and his All Stars continued their barnstorming tour and journeyed to Scranton, Pennsylvania; Lima, Ohio; Montreal, Canada; Atlantic Highlands, New Jersey; South Bend, Indiana; and Des Moines, Iowa. On October 16, Ruth played in an exhibition game in Kingston, New York, for the Kingston Colonials, in which he played first base and made three hits in four times at-bat. At that game, Ruth continued to show his unflinching support for handicapped and ill children when he presented an autographed baseball to a ten-year-old boy who was wheeled

Autographed baseball by Lou Gehrig sent to Johnny Sylvester in October of 1926. The ball was accompanied by a letter from Gehrig, in which the Yankee first baseman said the ball was the last one used in the 1926 World Series and he had been saving it, but he thought that Johnny would like it. The 1926 season was Gehrig's first full season as a Yankee, and he was on his way to playing 2,130 consecutive games. This record was later surpassed by Cal Ripkin Jr., who played in 2,632 consecutive games. *Brett Wood photo, courtesy of the Babe Ruth Birthplace and Museum and John Dale Sylvester Jr.*

to the ballpark and was suffering from infantile paralysis. The barnstorming tour ended at Iron Mountain, Michigan, on October 28.

Sunday, October 24, 1926, was a rainy windswept day in New York, and although seventy thousand people had shown up to see Grange when he first played in New York at the Polo Grounds, that day there was a crowd of only twenty thousand in the seats at the House that Ruth Built—Yankee

The tennis racquet given to Johnny Sylvester by "Big Bill" Tilden and inscribed: "To Johnnie—May you be a Champion.—William Tatem Tilden II. (Oct. 1926)." The racquet had been used by Tilden in the U.S. National Tennis Championships of 1926. *Courtesy of John Dale Sylvester Jr.*

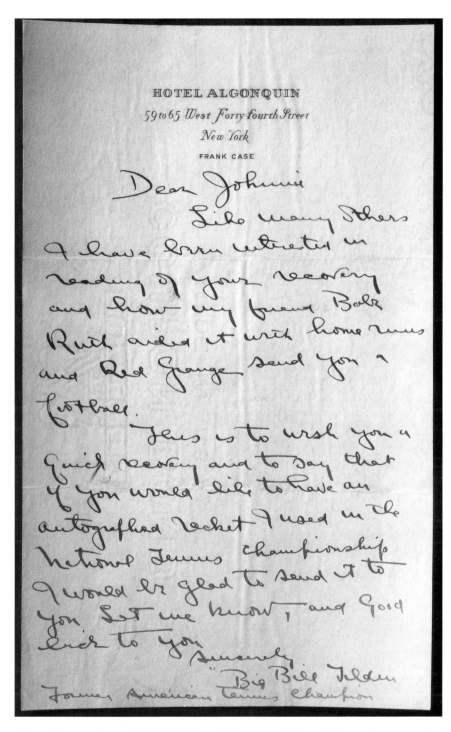

A letter from tennis star "Big Bill" Tilden offering to send Johnny Sylvester an autographed tennis racquet. *Johnny Sylvester Scrapbook.*

Stadium—who had braved the elements to see the football New York Yankees battle the Los Angeles Wildcats. It was the first time that Grange had played at Yankee Stadium. According to the *New York Times*, Grange "more than once threatened to sweep past the defense and down the field on one of his well-known jaunts," but it was not Grange but former Colgate star Eddie Tryon who scored the game's only touchdown in an eighty-yard run late in the game. Thus, Grange failed in his promised touchdown for Johnny Sylvester.

Sometime after Red Grange's autographed football arrived at Johnny's Essex Fells house, a letter came from "Big Bill" Tilden. He was, as he pointed out to Johnny in his letter, the former American tennis champion, having lost his title a few months before. In his letter, Tilden offered to send Johnny an autographed tennis racquet.

Apparently someone from the Sylvester household told Tilden that Johnny wanted the racquet, and on October 13, 1926, Johnny went to his door and found a package that contained a tennis racquet. It was autographed and sent by "Big Bill" Tilden, the world's leading tennis player, and it was the racquet he had used at the National Tennis Championships.

"Big Bill" was born William Tatem Tilden Jr. and at age twenty changed his name to William Tatem Tilden II, and changed the way the world looked at tennis for all time. During most of his career, he played amateur tennis and brought the sport from being an activity of the country club set similar to badminton to the sport of champion athletes that it is today.

Sportswriter Paul Gallico gave this description of Tilden:

> He stood six feet, one inch in his tennis socks and never weighed more than 165 ponds. He was built, if you ever saw him stripped in the locker room, along the lines of a gibbon—the wide shoulders which always seemed somewhat hunched, long, prehensile arms, flat, narrow waist and thin, caliper-like legs. His hair tended to sparseness on top, and he had a long nose and curiously heavy and prognathous jaw. But if you were designing a creature especially for the playing of big-league tennis, you could hardly improve upon Tilden's conformation—the elongated legs for covering the court in giant strides and the powerful shoulders and whiplash arms and wrists for flailing the ball.[91]

Amazingly, few knew at the time that Tilden played with a missing middle finger due to an amputation from an infection. He was flamboyant on and off the courts. Tilden lived in Philadelphia with his aunt during the off-seasons, but when he was in New York he made the Algonquin Hotel his home.

William Tatem Tilden II showing the form with which he dominated the tennis world during the 1920s. "Big Bill" Tilden was the first American male to win Wimbledon in 1920, won the United States amateur championship seven times—six times in succession—and led the United States Davis Cup team to seven consecutive victories. He is considered one of the greatest male tennis players of all time, but according to sportswriter Paul Gallico, "Of all the colorful champions of the era [Tilden] was far and away the oddest duck." *The New York Public Library.*

A cartoon by the great Harry W. Haenigsen that appeared in the *Dispatch* of Moline, Illinois, on October 14, 1926. Haenigsen had started out as a columnist and illustrator for the *New York Evening World* in 1919 and was a cartoonist and illustrator for over sixty years. In this cartoon he finds humor in the gifts given to make Johnny Sylvester well again. *Johnny Sylvester Scrapbook.*

Ruth's visit to the Sylvester home caught the eye of Charles Raymond Macauley (1871–1937), whose cartoons appeared in the country's leading newspapers for forty years. He originated the "Big Stick" associated with President Theodore Roosevelt, and in 1929 he won a Pulitzer Prize for a cartoon depicting World War I reparations. *Johnny Sylvester Scrapbook.*

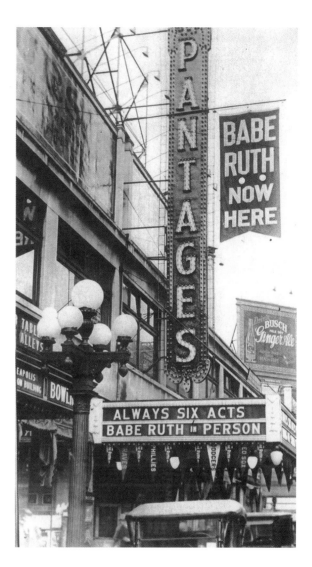

In November of 1926, Babe Ruth toured the west on the Pantages vaudeville circuit. Fellow teammate and Yankees' shortstop Mark Koenig saw the show in San Francisco with Tony Lazzeri and said it was "boring as hell." *Transcendental Graphics.*

After Tilden's racquet arrived at Johnny's house, Tilden wrote another letter to Johnny from his room at the Algonquin inviting the youngster and his parents to come to Wallack's Theatre in New York City to see the latest play Tilden was starring in, *They All Want Something Coming*, as his guests. Tilden suggested that a Wednesday or Saturday matinee might be the best performance for Johnny. He wrote Johnny that he should come backstage and then he could meet child actor Billy Quinn, age fourteen, who was starring with Tilden. *They All Want Something Coming* opened on October 12 and was a comedy written by Courtney Savage, based on a novel by E.J. Rath called *The Dark Chapter*. Besides Tilden and Quinn, the play featured

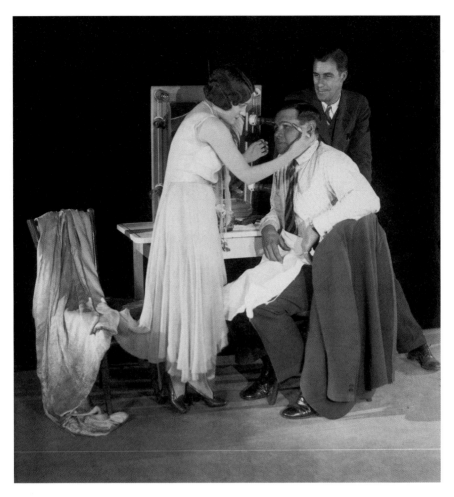

The Babe got makeup put on him by Gloria Swanson with tennis champion "Big Bill" Tilden looking on. In this photograph, taken on October 21, 1926, Babe was getting ready for a rehearsal of his upcoming vaudeville show on the Pantages circuit. *Bettmann/CORBIS.*

Katherine Revener and Charles S. Abbe. A *New York Times* critic called the play "elementary school entertainment" and of Tilden said, "He strikes a good many poses and manages to play about half of his scenes directly to the audience, enacting the role with none of the vitality that he shows on the tennis courts."[92] No one remembers if Johnny and his parents ever took Tilden up on his invitation.

Later in October, Essex Fells held its First Annual Pet Show. Johnny, apparently well recovered and back at school, won first prize in the rabbit class for his silver-gray rabbits.[93]

After his barnstorming tour ended at the end of October 1926, Ruth headed west to perform on the Pantages vaudeville circuit. The Pantages circuit was a collection of theaters owned or managed by Alexander Pantages, a Greek-born theatrical entrepreneur who had learned show business during the gold rush days when he teamed up with Klondike Kate Rockwell. By 1926, Pantages controlled all of the major theaters west of the Mississippi and was using them both for his favored vaudeville shows and also as movie houses. A typical vaudeville show would feature about ten acts—all of which were handpicked by Pantages himself.

Babe opened his vaudeville tour that year in Minneapolis. At the same time, Queen Marie of Rumania was visiting the same city on her tour of the United States, which was covered extensively by the national press. The Pantages people thought it would be a publicity coup if the Babe met the Queen and announced to her that he was the "King." Although the Associated Press reported that the Babe was going to meet Queen Marie, Ruth got involved with talking to a minor league player instead, missing the reception and the well-rehearsed publicity opportunity.[94]

Babe's contract for vaudeville guaranteed him $100,000 for a twelve-week tour on the Pantages circuit. Ruth's weekly take-home pay of over $8,000 was more than W.C. Fields, Fanny Brice or Al Jolson made. Ruth was a one-man show. He would enter the stage through a tissue paper hoop. He would toot on his saxophone, toss a baseball and tell a few jokes. Tony Lazzeri and Mark Koenig saw the show in San Francisco that year and Koenig said it was "boring as hell."[95] Ticket sales were lackluster. In between shows, Ruth endorsed Chevrolets, Packards, Cadillacs, Studebakers and Chryslers, as well as home appliances, boarding kennel and housing developments. After the vaudeville tour ended, Ruth stayed in Los Angeles for rehearsals for his starring role in *The Babe Comes Home.*

On December 16, 1926, Ruth wrote Johnny a handwritten letter on stationery from his vaudeville tour with letterhead that read, "The Pantages Theatre, Portland, Oregon." In the letter, Babe wished Johnny a Merry Christmas and a Happy New Year and concluded by saying, "You and I have a lot to remember about the 1926 World Series and when the Yanks win the championship next year I hope that you will be with me in person at the Stadium to help win another pennant."[96]

George D. Buckley, the man responsible for securing the baseballs that brought new health to Johnny Sylvester, wrote Johnny a full-page letter of encouragement on December 23, 1926. His letter included these paragraphs:

Babe Ruth and his young fans had a very special relationship, as witnessed by this photograph of the Babe taken during a break in his 1926 vaudeville tour at Vancouver, British Columbia. *Courtesy of the National Baseball Hall of Fame Library, Cooperstown, New York.*

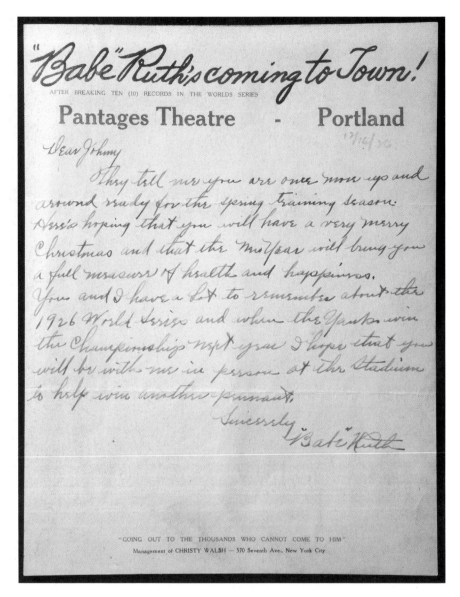

Babe Ruth's handwritten letter to Johnny Sylvester dated December 16, 1926, wishing Johnny a Merry Christmas and health and happiness in the New Year. According to Julia Ruth Stevens, her father rarely sent letters to anyone. *Johnny Sylvester Scrapbook.*

IT HAPPENS AFTER EVERY GAME

The second side of Babe Ruth's letter to Johnny Sylvester from the Pantages Theater in Portland, Oregon. *Johnny Sylvester Scrapbook.*

Yours was a great fight. We all watched it day by day. Sometimes we thought it was a shame that a good fighter like you had to have so much pain, but we always knew you would lick this trouble and when the time came, you would be back on the job of making everybody glad you were living.

Next to being able to put a good scrap is to know a fellow who can. While I have not seen Johnny Sylvester, I have seen how proudly his father told of the fight that Johnny was making and I have seen tears of joy spring into his eyes and I have envied that father and those friends who did know you.

Ruth continued visiting sick children in hospitals. According to sportswriter Fred Lieb, Ruth "was especially interested in the lame, the crippled and kids injured in accidents."[97] Lieb added that Ruth would usually tell them, "Hello kid, now you get well!" and would often close by saying, "I'll hit a homer for you tomorrow."[98]

On March 23, 1927, in a burlesque game between the Yankees and the Boston Braves in St. Petersburg, Florida, a small boy seated behind the Yankees' bench cried out at Ruth, "Come on, Babe, give us a homer." Babe turned to the boy and said, "Sure, kid, I'll sock a couple." Just to honor his pledge, Ruth knocked a homer in the sixth and in the eighth innings.[99]

Ford Frick, a former ghostwriter for the Christy Walsh syndicate who later became the commissioner of baseball, writes of an incident that occurred when the Yankees were barnstorming and had just arrived in Knoxville, Tennessee, after a tough ride from Nashville. According to Frick, most of the players went to their hotel rooms, including Ruth. Bob Meusel was the only player in the dining room of the hotel when an elderly Tennessee farmer approached him and asked him the whereabouts of Ruth. Meusel told him that "nobody ever knows but he had heard Ruth say he was going to his room." Meusel asked the man why he wanted to see Ruth. The farmer held up a fifty-cent "Rocket" baseball and said he wanted to obtain an autograph on it for his grandson, who was a young orphan living with his grandma. The boy had been counting the days until Ruth's arrival in town, but had contracted typhoid fever. The man said his grandson would be disappointed, but he would tell him that at least he tried. Meusel told him, "Hell, go pound on the door. He don't need too much sleep anyhow."

The next day Ruth was late in getting to the ballpark and completely missed batting practice because he had not only autographed the ball, but also had taken a taxi eighteen miles into the mountains to sit by the sick boy's side. Before he got there, he stopped to purchase some bats and a new glove for the boy. According to Frick, Meusel knew this story but didn't speak about it much. It never reached the papers. When Frick asked Ruth about it, Ruth told him, "He was a pretty nice kid. Guess he was pretty ill all right." When Frick asked what the name of the sick boy was Ruth replied, "Hell, I don't know. The old man called him 'son.' Guess I never did hear his name. If I did disremember. Never could remember names anyhow."

The story of Ruth healing a sick child was exceptional. But what curative powers did Ruth have? Paul Gallico, the sports editor for the *New York Daily News* from 1923 to 1936, probably observed Ruth more than any other writer. He wrote that "for a small boy to meet and touch him was to be suffused with the radiance and the glory, and the Babe even became endowed with powers of healing." Gallico went on to say that if "anyone should be looking to canonize a saint of baseball there are authentic records, all during our times, of Ruth saving the life of this or that sick child by a hospital bedside visit and the promise to hit a home run especially for him, and one which he always managed to keep."[100]

Sportswriter Fred Lieb wrote of one incident that occurred in Phillips Field, Tampa, Florida. In this story, a man had a sick son who two years before had lost his ability to walk and could not even stand up. The boy became a big Babe Ruth fan and read everything he could about the Bambino. When the boy read that Ruth was going to appear with the Yankees at Phillips Field, he had his father drive him to the game. The father got permission to actually drive his car right next to the right field foul line. All of the players had to pass this location in order to return to the bus. Ruth walked by the open window and said, "Hi'ya kid!" The boy, full of joy, suddenly jumped up to return the greeting. The boy's father was ecstatic, with tears running down his face. He screamed, "I'm so happy I can hardly speak. It's two years since my boy could stand up!" The story was confirmed by Leo Durocher, who was a rookie infielder at the time.[101] Babe corroborated the story in *The Babe Ruth Story* and wrote, "I worked a miracle that spring at Tampa."[102] This story would be portrayed in the movie of the same name.

Because of what Ruth did for Johnny Sylvester and other sick children, Paul Gallico actually canonized Ruth in a fictional short story written about ten years after Ruth's death. The story was called "Saint Bambino."

According to sportswriter Tom Meany, when the Yankees first visited Philadelphia in 1927, a well-dressed middle-aged man introduced himself as Johnny Sylvester's uncle and said to Ruth, "I thought you'd like to know, Mr. Ruth, that Johnny is making a remarkable recovery. He certainly would want to thank you and I want to thank you on behalf of the family."

"That's fine," replied the Babe. "I'm certainly glad to hear it. You tell Johnny I was asking for him and telling him to keep up the good work." They shook hands and parted. Babe gazed after the older man left, scratched his head and murmured, "Now who the hell is Johnny Sylvester?"

But the truth was that Ruth was terrible with proper names. He usually called anyone under thirty "Kid" and anyone over thirty "Doc."

Once right before Ruth was to have dinner with the leading film stars of the day, Ruth told someone, "I'm having dinner with those movie people." To which a friend replied, "You mean Mary Pickford and Douglas Fairbanks Jr.?" "Yes," Ruth replied.

Ruth would also mix up newspaper reporters and their newspapers. Once in 1934, sportswriter Charles (Mike) Houston, his wife and sister-in-law paid a visit to Ruth and his wife at Washington's Shoreham Hotel. Ruth was staying at the hotel while the Yankees were playing a series with the Senators. Houston worried that Ruth wouldn't remember him from a year before. He left pleased as punch that Ruth and his wife had entertained him for over an hour. The next day, Ruth told members of the press, "You'll never guess who came up to visit us last night—Smitty!" He was referring to Ken Smith of the *Daily Mirror*.

Ruth established the all-time season home run record of sixty home runs in 1928. The record would last for some thirty years until Roger Maris hit sixty-one in 1960 in an expanded season. In 1928, Ruth made headlines when he paid youngster Lennie Beals twenty dollars for his sixtieth home run ball. The ball is now part of the Babe Ruth collection at the Baseball Museum and Hall of Fame in Cooperstown, New York. The pitcher who hurled the ball to Ruth for his sixtieth home run was Tom Zachary of the Washington Senators on the final day of the season. After the game, Zachary came into the Yankee clubhouse and congratulated Ruth. When he left Ruth asked, "Who the hell was that?"

Johnny Sylvester would have the last laugh on the incident when years later at his tenth reunion at Princeton University he held up a sign that read, "Who the hell is Babe Ruth?"

Chapter Four

I expect to make myself a better man, physically, mentally and morally.
—Johnny Sylvester

As baseball season approached in 1927, fans throughout the country wanted to know whether the boy who had been saved by Babe Ruth's home runs would be attending opening day ceremonies at Yankee Stadium. The night before the big day, Mrs. Horace Sylvester announced that her son would not be making the game because he wasn't feeling too well and she felt the weather was too chilly. She stated that Johnny was "pulling" for his old sponsor Babe Ruth to return to his home run form.

April 12, 1927, a gorgeous day in the Bronx, saw seventy-two thousand fans pack Yankee Stadium for the opening day game between the Yankees and the Philadelphia Athletics. Another twenty-five thousand fans were turned away by police. It surpassed the previous attendance record set at the second game of the 1926 World Series. At 3:15 p.m., the players marched to center field and saw the stars and stripes raised, along with the 1926 American League pennant flag. Mayor Jimmy Walker threw out the ceremonial first pitch. Among the celebrities present were Sir Thomas Lipton, who sat with Colonel Ruppert in the owner's box; Dr. Wilhelm Cuno, the former chancellor of the German Republic; and songwriter George M. Cohan.

Many were predicting that the Philadelphia Athletics would win the pennant in 1927. Connie Mack, the clever manager of the Athletics, had assembled a top-flight team, with outstanding pitchers including Lefty Grove, Rube Walberg and Eddie Rommel. He also had Mickey Cochrane, one of the league's best catchers, and forty-year-old Ty Cobb. Upon joining the Athletics, Cobb said, "I regret that I am not ten years younger, but I promise you that I will give Mr. Mack the best I am physically able to do."[103] The presence of Cobb and Ruth on opening day accounted for most of the fans, and as the two great baseball players posed together for pictures, James R. Harrison of the *New York Times* reported that "there were so many photographers on the field that it looked like a national convention of the Photographers' Union."[104] While Ty Cobb got a bunt and scored a run, it was not a good day for the Babe and the Yankees. Ruth struck out twice, popped out and then left the game in the sixth inning feeling dizzy. The Yankees lost to the Athletics by a score of 8–2.

After the game, Johnny was contacted and when asked about Ruth's performance he said, "He did fine." He added that his father hadn't wanted him to miss school and that he wasn't quite strong enough to attend a game. According to author Weldon in his book *Babe Ruth*, "The game had meaning for Johnny Sylvester, too. It was to have meant the second happiest day of his life, spent actually watching the Babe play. But he had a cold that day, and the trip to the Bronx had to be put off for a week."[105] But Johnny did receive a telephone call from Ruth after the game, in which Ruth promised to visit him within a few days.

On June 18, 1927, St. Louis held a Lindbergh Day celebration. Charles A. Lindbergh, who less than a year before had been flying mail pouches on the perilous route between St. Louis and Chicago, flew his *Spirit of St. Louis* to Lambert Field, the field he knew so well. This time, however, Lindbergh was the conquering hero and 500,000 people had turned out to salute him in a citywide parade. He then went to Sportsman's Park, where he honored the 1926 Cardinals by raising their pennant flag and presenting each of the players from the 1926 Cardinals with a World Series ring.

As the Babe had promised Johnny Sylvester in 1926, the New York Yankees won the pennant in 1927. That year, Ruth hit his record-breaking sixty home runs and "Murderers' Row" became a household expression.

Johnny Sylvester would continue to be in the public's eye in 1928. In March, a photograph of Johnny playing golf with his father in Pinehurst, North Carolina, appeared in newspapers all over the country. A few days earlier, his father had purchased land in Southern Pines.

Having missed the opening day ceremonies for the Yankees in 1927, Johnny was in attendance when the Yankees opened the season on April 20, 1928. On hand again was popular New York City Mayor Jimmy Walker to throw out the first pitch. On the center field flagpole beside the American flag, the American League Championship Pennant and the 1927 World Series Championship Pennant were both raised. Each member of the 1927 team was presented with a diamond-studded World Series ring.

On Saturday, June 18, 1927, thirty-five days after leaving from Lambert Field, St. Louis, on his world-shattering transatlantic flight, Charles A. Lindbergh returned to that field in his single-engine *Spirit of St. Louis* to raise the Cardinals' 1926 championship pennant at Sportsman's Park. A crowd of thirty thousand people saw him present the 1926 World Series rings to the team. Rogers Hornsby, who was traded after the '26 season to the New York Giants, is seen in his gray Giants uniform with Commissioner Kenesaw Mountain Landis standing by. *Courtesy of the Missouri Historical Society.*

Johnny posed with the Babe, and a classic photograph of the boy and his savior appeared on the cover of the *Sporting News*,[106] as well as in the *Brooklyn Eagle* and scores of other newspapers throughout the country. It was also framed and accorded a place of honor in Johnny Sylvester's house.

As was the case the year before, on opening day the Yankees played the Athletics, Ruth went hitless and the Yankees lost 2–1, this time before a crowd of fifty-five thousand.

In the 1928 World Series, the New York Yankees again faced the St. Louis Cardinals. In the first game, pitcher Waite Hoyt held the Cardinals to three hits and Babe hit two doubles, helping the Yankees to win the game by a score of 3–1.

In the second game, Ruth hit a double and a single, and the Yankees atoned for 1926 and beat Grover Cleveland Alexander and the Cardinals by a score of 9–3.

Johnny Sylvester and Babe Ruth during opening day ceremonies at Yankee Stadium on April 20, 1928, where fifty-five thousand fans showed up. Johnny had missed the ceremonies in 1927 that drew an unbelievable seventy-two thousand fans, but he received a personal telephone call from Ruth after the game. Sporting News/*ZUMA Press.*

The series then moved to St. Louis. In the third game, Babe hit two singles and had a hard-hitting slide into the catcher, which caused him to drop the ball and the Cardinals to slip behind so they never caught up. The Yankees won 7–3 behind the pitching of Tom Zachary.

In the fourth game at Sportsman's Park, Ruth hit a home run to tie the score 1–1 in the fourth inning. In the seventh inning, Bill Sherdel fired two rapid strikes to Ruth. Then, as Ruth was arguing with the umpire, the Cardinal catcher Jimmie Wilson quickly threw the ball back to Sherdel, who returned it almost immediately. The umpire ruled that the pitch was a "quick pitch," which was allowed in the National League, disallowed in the American League and not allowed by consent in the World Series. The umpire allowed another pitch, which Ruth clobbered for his second home run over the right field pavilion.

In the eighth inning, Grover Cleveland Alexander came in to relieve Sherdel. This time Babe made up for his 1926 performance against Alexander and hit him for his third home run. It was the second time in a World Series that he had hit three home runs in one game. This record has never been broken. The fans at Sportsman's Park realized the momentous occasion and gave him an even bigger ovation than they had in 1926. James Harrison of the *New York Times* wrote, "If there is any lingering doubt, if anywhere in this broad land there were misguided souls who believed that Babe Ruth was not the greatest living ballplayer, they should have seen him today."[107] The Babe had batted .625 during the series with ten hits during sixteen at-bats, nine runs scored and three homers in one game for the second time. It was the best World Series game of Ruth's career.

For his first year of high school, Johnny attended the Kingsley School in Essex Fells, New Jersey. According to school records, Johnny was "industrious, reliable and highly trustworthy." At Kingsley, Johnny played football, baseball and ice hockey. During his year there he was troubled by a sinus condition that necessitated surgery. His class ranking for the year was second out of fifteen.

For his last three years of high school, Sylvester attended Montclair Academy in Montclair, New Jersey, which was a college preparatory country day and boarding school for boys from first grade to college. At Montclair Academy, he served as secretary on the student council, was a member of Rostrum and the Honor Committee and during his junior year ran the junior prom.

Johnny played center on the ice hockey team and was the team's captain during his senior year. That year he led the team with goals scored, at eleven. In the academy's yearbook in 1933, Johnny was lauded for his "capable and inspiring leadership" that made the team "one of the most successful that Montclair Academy has ever produced."[108]

Johnny's father, Horace Sylvester, helped to make National City Company one of the largest originating and distributing organizations for state, county, municipal and provincial bonds in the United States. Horace worked closely with Charles E. Mitchell, former chairman of the affiliated First National Bank, and became known as a top-notch salesman in the municipal field. In 1924, he won recognition by landing a $67,400,000 issue of New York City bonds against savage competition. The following year he negotiated a $500,000,000 bond deal.

Horace introduced to investors bonds of the Federal Land Banks and of the Port of New York Authority. The Port of New York Authority had been created in 1921 as a regional political entity for the development of the more than eight hundred miles of waterfront. It was called by that name until 1972, when it was renamed the Port Authority of New York and New Jersey. Working with the authority, the brilliant Swiss engineer Othmar H. Amman was responsible for the George Washington Bridge, the Bayonne Bridge and the Verrazano-Narrows Bridge. The projects that it developed were not built at taxpayers' expense but by the issuance of tax-exempt bonds. The bonds would be repaid by the tolls that would later be collected. In 1933, Archibald McLeish called it "one of the most interesting and potentially one of the most formidable political agencies America has yet produced."[109]

In 1929, Horace relocated his family to the nearby town of North Caldwell, purchasing for $100,000 a huge Federalist-style estate with twenty-six rooms. Mr. Sylvester purchased it after it was certain that Colonel Charles A. Lindbergh was not negotiating for it. On July 25, 1929, Alexander H. Sands Jr., an official of the British American Tobacco Company, announced that there was "nothing" to the report that Lindbergh was engaged in negotiating to purchase the estate on a hill close to the new flying field being developed by the Curtiss Flying Service.[110] Lindbergh instead purchased land in South Jersey and built a home in Hopewell, New Jersey. In 1932, Charles A. Lindbergh Jr. was kidnapped from the Hopewell home, and his body was later found in a shallow grave not far from the home.

While living in his estate in North Caldwell, Horace established the Sylvan Crest Kennels, where he bred setters and spaniels. He kept tropical fish and even some wild animals but his pride and joy was his tropical bird collection. One of his favorite birds was a macaw named Charlie.

In 1931, Horace became vice-president in charge of the sales department at the National City Company. When he was appointed, the company praised "his ability and intimate knowledge of the organization."[111]

Home of Horace C. Sylvester Jr. and family, located in North Caldwell, New Jersey. It was reported in the *Caldwell Progress* that in 1929 Horace C. Sylvester paid $100,000 for this twenty-six-room mansion. *Photo by the author.*

Horace was never questioned for the millions of dollars in bonds that he handled, but the United States Senate Banking and Currency Committee on March 2, 1933, took testimony in regard to a certain loan that had been listed as an expense on the books of Sylvester's company. The Senate Committee, through its chief counsel, Ferdinand Pecora, presented testimony concerning an unsecured loan for $10,200 made by the First National City Company to John E. Ramsey, general manager of the Port of New York Authority. Testifying before the committee was Edward F. Barrett, vice-president of the National City Bank. Barrett testified that in June of 1931 Ramsey had come to him in a financial jam and asked him for a loan. According to Barrett, Ramsey signed a personal note to him (which he misplaced) agreeing to pay the money back, plus interest. Barrett then took Ramsey upstairs to Horace Sylvester and informed him of Ramsey's plight and instructed him to advance the money to Ramsey. Sylvester directed the company treasurer, Samuel W. Baldwin, to issue the check, cash it and show it on the books of the syndicate as an expense. Sylvester had handled the National City Company $66 million bond issue for the Port of Authority of New York six weeks earlier.

Horace Sylvester testified next. When asked by Pecora if the loan to Ramsey was unusual, he replied that over the past ten years over $4,500,000,000 of municipal bonds had come through his hands and there had never been a similar loan, but he also testified that every manager of a bond fund has an amount set aside for expenses and from that fund the loan money was paid. According to the *New York Times*, Mr. Sylvester pounded the table and vehemently denied that the loan to the general manager had given First National Company an unfair advantage over its competitors, pointing out that the loan was not made until June 3 and that the bond issue had been completely sold to the public by April 22.[112]

The next day the New York district attorney ordered a criminal investigation. On March 21, 1933, a New York County grand jury handed down an indictment against Horace Sylvester, charging him with forgery in the third degree in ordering a false entry in the books of the First National Company. If convicted, Sylvester faced a prison term of between two and a half and five years. He came to his arraignment with his lawyer, George V. Olvany, former leader of Tammany Hall, and according to the *New York Times*, Sylvester appeared at his arraignment "unperturbed and smiling through most of the proceeding."[113]

Mr. Sylvester tendered his resignation to the company, but the directors of National City Company, believing in the innocence of Sylvester, declined to accept it. Sylvester continued on as head of the sales department when the company became City Company of New York in June. Ramsey also offered his resignation to the Port Authority, but it was declined by Chairman John F. Galvin, who ordered his own investigation. On April 11, 1933, the Port Authority commissioners exonerated Mr. Ramsey of any wrongdoing in connection with the loan.

While his father was going through the criminal courts, young John Sylvester continued his studies at Montclair Academy and applied to Princeton University. In his essay submitted for admission, he stated that he had long held the college "in the greatest admiration." Some of the things that attracted him to it were "the warmth and beauty of the campus, the excellence in hockey, my favorite sport and the reputation the graduates enjoy." As to what he would gain by a course at Princeton, Johnny wrote, "I expect to make myself a better man, physically, mentally and morally."

Just as he had in 1926, Johnny's father reached out to another one of his colleagues at the First National City Bank to write a letter of support for his son. This time his friend was Gordon S. Rentschler, who had been president of his 1907 Princeton graduating class and was now president of one of the largest banks in the world, having obtained the presidency at age forty-three. In 1933, Rentschler served as chairman of the New York

JOHN SYLVESTER

Age 18, Weight 130, Height 5 ft. 6 in.

Years at M. A.—3

Activities 1930-31: Rostrum, Hockey Team. 1931-32: Junior Prom Committee, Hockey Team. 1932-33: Captain of the Hockey Team, Honor Committee, Secretary of Rostrum, Secretary of Student Council, Chairman of Rostrum-Forum Dance Committee.

Meet the diminutive but able captain of the hockey team, chairman of the Rostrum-Forum Dance Committee, member of the Rostrum, who stands third in his class: John Sylvester. A walking example of the fact that little men can do big things, Johnny last year was instrumental in putting over a good Junior Prom. He seems perfectly satisfied in being chairman of the dance committee, a job most of us would not relish, and still finds time to be all over the ice at once. Johnny is one of those who will need no luck at all to succeed easily in college.

PRINCETON

Johnny Sylvester's senior class photograph and caption from *Ye Yearbook* of Montclair Academy, 1933. *Courtesy of Montclair-Kimberly Academy Archives.*

Clearing House Committee during the turbulent and historic days of the bank holiday. At the end of May 1933, Johnny's father sent Rentschler a copy of a newspaper article that had appeared in the *Montclair Times* relating that Johnny was graduating from Montclair Academy *cum laude*. On June 3, 1933, Rentschler wrote a letter in support of Johnny. Princeton responded almost immediately and advised him that they were aware of Johnny's outstanding academic record at Montclair Academy and would keep him updated on Johnny's application.

On Friday, June 9, 1933, Johnny attended Montclair Academy's commencement ceremonies at Montclair's Unity Church, graduating third out of a class of thirty-three.

Johnny entered Princeton University in the fall of 1933, majoring in economics. He did not disappoint the administration and during his freshman year he was one of the top ten students in his class.

While Johnny was achieving continued academic excellence at Princeton, there was good news for his father. In October, the indictment against his father was dismissed by Judge Freschi of New York's General Sessions Court with a ruling indicating that no crime had been committed, since there was no larceny and no one had been defrauded. The judge ruled that the monies came not from the syndicate but from the reserves set aside for sundries of the First National City Company. After the decision was announced, the City Company of New York issued a statement on behalf of the directors stating that they were satisfied with the innocence of Mr. Sylvester and had continued him as a vice-president. As for Ramsey, he would continue on as the general manager of the Port Authority until his retirement in 1942.

In April 1934, Charles E. Mitchell, one of Wall Street's top bondsmen—who had worked closely with "Syl," as Horace was known on Wall Street—was testifying in a case brought by minority stockholders against the directors of National City Bank. Mitchell's position, which was upheld by the court, was that for a bank to hold onto top-level men they had to be offered some profit-sharing plans. Upon cross-examination, Mitchell was asked about the duties of Mr. Sylvester. His reply was as follows: "As I told you yesterday, Mr. Sylvester was a man who came over with the N.W. Halsey organization. His duties particularly had to do with municipal, state and government finance and he is in my opinion—that does not mean very much to you, perhaps—but in my opinion he is the top of all municipal bond experts in the United States."[114]

An indication of just how scrupulous Johnny's father really was came in the winter of 1934. When Horace received Johnny's superb report card from Princeton, the envelope also contained a statement of the regulations forbidding students at Princeton to drive on campus. Horace wrote a

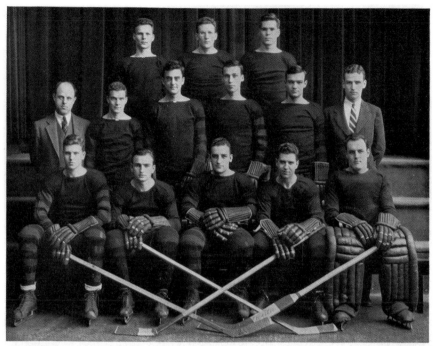

TOP ROW: Cook, Covey, Burke. SECOND ROW: Vaughan (Coach), Sylvester, Stonington, Potter, Woodhull, Edwards (Mgr.). FRONT ROW Barrett, Bissell, Willis (Capt.), Lawson, Gregory.

Johnny Sylvester with his teammates on the 1937 Princeton varsity hockey team. He is pictured here in the middle row, second from left, next to Coach Vaughan. In a game on February 12, 1935, Sylvester scored a "hat trick" when he made three goals as a wing in a game against the Boston College Eagles. *Princeton University Archives.*

letter to the dean stating that he was pleased with Johnny's report card but inquiring whether Johnny had ever broken the driving regulations. He stated in his letter to the dean that he was very concerned that his son should not in any way break any rules or regulations. He pointed out to the dean that Johnny owned a car and often came home on Saturdays and returned to the Princeton campus on Mondays, and that he was usually accompanied by his mother, Miss Murray (Johnny's girlfriend) or the chauffeur. Johnny's companion would take the wheel at Princeton Airport and then drive Johnny to the campus. The dean responded that the procedure Johnny was following was not in any way an infringement on the driving regulations.

For three years at Princeton, Johnny was on the varsity ice hockey team. In a game that was to be the highlight of his collegiate hockey career, on February 12, 1935, little Johnny, as a second-string wing, scored a hat trick and led the Princeton Tigers to a 6–1 victory over the Boston College Eagles. Sylvester scored his first goal in the fourteen minutes of the first period and then scored a goal in the second period with a pretty backhand shot. A minute later he scored his third goal by stickhandling his way to the hash marks from the crease on a hard shot. The game was Princeton's sixth victory of the season and the first defeat in six games for the Eagles. It would be said by some that Johnny never played hockey without a helmet on account of his 1926 injury.

In his sophomore year at Princeton, Johnny made the second group Bachelor of Arts Honor Roll and had his name published by the *New York Times* on July 24, 1935, after the school year had ended. He was the intramural manager in Cannon Club. His Princeton senior thesis was entitled "A Quantitative Study of the Factors Affecting the Automotive Demand for Gasoline in the State of New Jersey."

The year 1935 would be the Babe's last year playing Major League baseball. But just as he had done in 1926, he dedicated a home run. It was on April 16 at a Red Sox–Yankees game in Fenway Park. Governor Louis J. Brann of Maine presented the Babe with a Maine fishing license at the game. The governor then told Babe, "You know, Mr. Ruth, I've never seen you hit a home run!" "Is that so," replied the Babe. "Well, well, I'll attend to that. I'll hit one for you the next time I come up." And he did—a 430-foot drive into the runway between the right field grandstand and bleachers.[115]

The National City Company became the City Company and was dissolved in 1935. At that point Horace joined Brown, Harriman & Co. as a vice-president. He stayed with the company when it became Harriman, Ripley & Co. with offices at 63 Wall Street in New York City.

Johnny graduated from Princeton University in 1937, and immediately went to work for the personal trust department of Guaranty Trust Company in New York City. He left that firm and went to work in 1939 as a brokerage clerk for Laurence M. Marks & Company with offices located at 49 Wall Street in New York City. He kept active with his Princeton alumni and served as secretary of the Princeton Alumni Association of Montclair, New Jersey, from 1939 to 1940.

In November 1940, Johnny left Marks & Company and entered a packaging business run by his uncle. Also in 1940, Horace Sylvester placed his palatial North Caldwell estate on the market and moved his family back to Essex Fells.

On February 3, 1941, Horace, as was his routine, woke up at 5:00 a.m. and went to the basement recreation room of his home. There he made coffee and fed his tropical birds. He then took a 20-gauge shotgun and shot himself. The shot was heard by his butler, Arthur Clark, who called the police

Johnny Sylvester as he appeared in his senior class photograph from Princeton University in 1937. *Princeton University Archives.*

and a doctor. Clark, his wife and Horace's mother-in-law Lilly Keenan were the only ones in the house at the time. Horace's wife and daughter were away in Harrisburg, Pennsylvania, and had spoken to him the night before. Johnny and his brothers, Horace III and Peter, were all in New York at the time. Horace left a note that read, "No funeral, just cremation."

During his forty years in municipal bond work, observers stated that he had handled billions of dollars. An official at Harriman, Ripley suggested to the press that the suicide was caused by a combination of illnesses and "conditions of business and war and everything else."[116] This was a tragic end to the man who had brought the great Babe Ruth into his son's life in order to save him. Horace C. Sylvester Jr. was fifty-seven years of age.

Chapter Five

He's one great guy!
—Johnny Sylvester

I consider Mr. Sylvester a gentleman of the very highest character, far above the average mentality, and I believe he would in every way make a most desirable officer of the United States Navy," wrote Laurence M. Marks, the head of the Wall Street firm of the same name, on March 17, 1942. His letter was addressed to the commandant of the Third Naval District in New York City in support of Johnny's application for a commission.

On July 4, 1942, Johnny Sylvester entered active naval duty as an apprentice seaman. He went on to attend the twelve-week course at the U.S. Navy's Midshipmen's School and received training on the USS *Prairie State*, the navy training "houseboat" anchored in the Hudson River at 135th Street. The *Prairie State* was the former *Illinois*, a battleship that had been commissioned in 1901 and served as part of Teddy Roosevelt's White Fleet. The navy established the school in 1940, and by early 1941 it had incorporated a series of Columbia University buildings for its programs. The aim was to produce naval officers in just three months. Johnny considered himself "a ninety-day wonder."[117] Sylvester completed the Midshipmen's School on October 28, 1942, and was commissioned an ensign.

Johnny's further naval training included ten weeks at the University of Illinois for diesel engineering, eight weeks at the Submarine Chaser Training Center in Miami, Florida, and two weeks at the navy's sound school in Key West, Florida.

For the next three and a half years Johnny toured on several naval ships in the Pacific theater and rose to full lieutenant commanding submarine chaser 520. The navy, as it did with its PT boats, gave numbers to its subchasers, and Johnny's ship was officially known as SC-520. It was of

Johnny Sylvester married his childhood sweetheart, Marita Murray, on shore leave from the navy on October 29, 1942. *Courtesy of John Dale Sylvester Jr.*

the SC-497 class. In that class were 580 wooden-hulled, 110-foot boats that were built during World War II; 142 of the submarine chasers had been given to the Allies under the Lend-Lease program. Johnny's ship was built by the Vineyard Shipbuilding Co. of Milford, Delaware, launched on April 18, 1942, and commissioned on May 25, 1942. The ship carried one 40-millimeter gun forward, three antiaircraft guns in the midsection and a twin 50-caliber machine gun aft. The ship was serviced by a complement of twenty-seven: three officers and twenty-four enlisted men. The subchasers were designed for offshore patrols and anti-submarine warfare. They were constructed to fight the German U-boats that were operating off the Atlantic Coast. In the Pacific theater, they were used for amphibious landings and as escorts.

Johnny's command of SC-520 was in the Hawaiian Sea Frontier, where his ship escorted other naval vessels and performed soundings for Japanese submarines around the Hawaiian Islands. He commanded his ship on trips to Christmas Island, Palmyra atoll and Canton Island. On Canton Island, which is roughly halfway between Hawaii and Fiji, the navy had constructed a six-thousand-foot runway that was used for stopovers for flights to Australia and New Zealand and also as a staging ground for attacks on the Japanese-held Gilbert Islands.

On October 29, 1942, while on shore duty, Johnny Sylvester married Marita Murray of Bloomfield, New Jersey. Marita had been Johnny's first and only girlfriend and had grown up with him in Essex Fells.

Johnny's mother Helen Sylvester, without Horace's financial assistance, started operating a tearoom in Caldwell, New Jersey, called the Hitching Post. It was a small tearoom that served lunches and dinners. It was located in an eighteenth-century house, and its name derived from the presence of a colonial hitching post in front. Patrons were always impressed by a cageless macaw named Charlie. After his mother died, Johnny took over ownership of the Hitching Post in Caldwell and moved his grandmother, two of his aunts and two cousins into rooms in the building.

Johnny ended his naval service in August of 1945 at the U.S. Personnel Separation Center in Lido Beach, New York, and resumed working at Amsco Packaging Machinery Company in Long Island City, New York.

April 27, 1947, was declared to be "Babe Ruth Day" in all leagues in the United States and Japan. In anticipation of the great event, public interest again focused on the story of Babe Ruth and Johnny Sylvester.

On April 15, 1947, Johnny received a letter from the producers of the *Readers Digest Radio Edition*, which had a television show that aired on Thursdays from 10:00 p.m. until 10:30 p.m. The producers sought Johnny's

Charlie, a macaw that was in the collection of Horace C. Sylvester Jr., later made his home in the Hitching Post and finally ended up on the wall in Johnny Sylvester's Garden City, Long Island home. *Photo by the author.*

permission to use an actor to portray him for a television show to be broadcast on April 24 over the Columbia Broadcasting System.

Jinx Falkenburg of the *Tex and Jinx* radio show knew that the real Johnny Sylvester would be better than any actor, and she telegrammed Johnny on April 23, 1947, stating that "we would like very much to have you appear on our radio program to tell the Babe Ruth story on Monday May 5."[118]

According to sportswriter Tom Meany, the idea of having Johnny Sylvester and Babe Ruth be reunited was the brainstorm of Rae Wilmer, the managing editor of the *Newspaper PM*—later the *New York Star*, a revolutionary newspaper without advertising that was owned by the eccentric Chicago millionaire Marshall Fields III. Wilmer thought it would be a great public interest story if Sylvester could be located and brought to the Babe during the Babe's eighty-two-day hospital stay in French Hospital in New York. At that point, no one knew exactly how ill the Babe was and the visit was not permitted, since Ruth's hospital room had a strict "no visitors" policy. Press reports covered his hospitalization and mentioned surgery on his neck, but no one really knew the extent of his illness.

Through the auspices of the *Daily News*, Johnny Sylvester was able to have a reunion meeting with the Babe—some twenty-one years after his first meeting. It happened on April 26, 1947. The place was Ruth's apartment located at 110 Riverside Drive, New York City. Ruth and his wife Claire had moved into the eleven-room apartment in 1942. Tour guides on the Circle Line boats would often take their passengers up the Hudson River and point out the large Italianate apartment building where the Big Bambino lived.

Johnny and his wife Marita arrived at the apartment and were let in by a nurse. The following description of the visit was captured by a reporter for the *New York Daily News* who filed an eyewitness account. While waiting nervously in the Babe's living room, Johnny told Marita, "I hope he remembers me."

Just then, wearing pajamas and a robe, tanned from his recent Florida stay, Babe Ruth entered the living room, broke out in a big smile and said, "Hello Johnny. The last time I saw you, you were a skinny little kid." He then grasped Johnny's hand warmly. Johnny, seemingly again in awe of the Babe, responded, "Hello Babe, I'm grown up now, thanks to you."

The Babe nodded and had Johnny and his wife sit down on the sofa. The Babe then told Johnny and Marita about his recent illness. Smiling, Johnny told the Babe, "Well, Babe, it's only right that I should visit you, after what you did for me, twenty-one years ago."

Johnny would later comment that "Ruth was obviously a very sick man who had lost a lot of weight and he looked very gaunt sitting in his pajamas and bathrobe."[119]

At that point, Johnny took out the two baseballs that Ruth had sent him in 1926 and said, "I thought you'd like to see these, sir." "Let's see 'em," replied Ruth, who examined them closely. "Oh yes, Meusel, Koenig—they were great boys," he murmured.

"When you sent these baseballs to me you were really making dents in them, Babe," laughed Johnny. "Yes," Babe muttered to himself, "those were great days."

While posing for photographs, Babe and Johnny discussed golf. Babe told Johnny about his adventures in Southern golf courses. They chatted about divots and sand traps. The Babe told Johnny he had just returned from bowling, which he had been playing in order to get his strength back. The talk then focused on what Babe was doing for American Legion baseball on behalf of the Ford Motor Company.

Babe then looked at Johnny and said, "I want to get all the kids out—if the kids don't play baseball, the game has no future. The only way to keep a stream of stars coming into the Majors is to get them when they're

Johnny Sylvester, in order to lift the spirits of his savior, returned to visit Ruth at his Riverside Drive apartment in New York City on April 26, 1947, bringing with him the two autographed baseballs that were sent to him from St. Louis. Ruth is seen holding the ball on which he promised to hit the homer for Johnny in the fourth game of the 1926 World Series. New York Daily News.

young, have them like the game and develop them—then baseball will have something."

Johnny and Marita knew it was time to wind up their visit. Johnny told the Babe, "Well, Babe, thank you for letting me see you again. I want you to know that there wasn't any difference between this visit and the last—it's been a thrill!" Ruth replied, "I've gotten a great kick out of having you come to see me, son."

As the door to Babe's apartment was closing, Johnny looked back and said, "He's one great guy."

On October 5, 1947, Johnny received a letter from the advertising company of Batten, Barton, Durstine & Osborn, Inc. enclosing a script and seeking his permission to use actors to portray himself and his father in another television production entitled *Big Boy: The Story of Babe Ruth*, written by Brice Disque Jr. The letter pointed out that Babe Ruth had no objection. *Big Boy* was broadcast on the *Cavalcade of America* on October 6, 1947.

The first major motion picture of Ruth's life was *The Babe Ruth Story* in 1948, starring William Bendix as the Babe. The movie was almost universally panned by the critics. The movie featured the Johnny Sylvester story but with two glaring errors—it had Ruth promising to hit home runs for Johnny while visiting him in a hospital before the World Series. Johnny was never in a hospital and his visit by Ruth came after the series was over. Also, instead of Essex Fells, New Jersey, the town Johnny was supposedly living in was Gary, Indiana.

On October 19, 1947, Brother Gilbert, the Xaverian brother who was responsible for bringing Ruth into baseball by introducing him to Jack Dunn of the Baltimore Orioles,, died while saying his prayers at Keith Academy in Lowell, Massachusetts. In 1914, Dunn had made Ruth an offer to play baseball for $600 per year. Ruth would later say, "I had some great moments in the years that followed that, including the day I signed a contract for $80,000 a year with the New York Yankees. But none of my later thrills ever topped the one I got that cold afternoon at St. Mary's when $600 seemed to me to be all the wealth in the world."[120] Learning that Ruth was too ill to attend the funeral, a ten-year-old boy sent Babe the following letter:

> *I'm sorry your friend died.*
> *If you wish and the Brothers, will let children go to the mass, I will go for*
> *you as I live in Danvers.*
> *I will behave.*
> *Love,*
> *Frank Haggerty.*

Babe sent the following telegram back to young Frank:

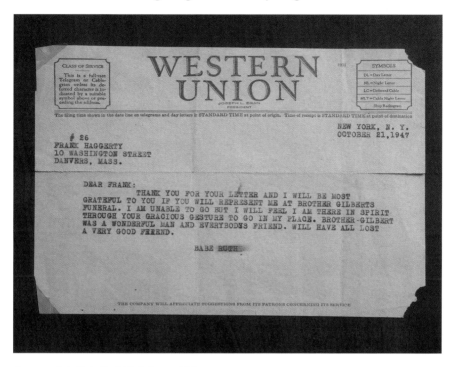

Courtesy of the Babe Ruth Birthplace and Museum.

Although he was seriously ill through most of 1947, the Babe continued to champion causes that benefited children. He served as a roving ambassador for the Ford Motor Company in support of American Legion baseball.

On August 16, 1948, at 8:01 p.m., Babe Ruth died in his sleep. Outside of Memorial Hospital, twelve-year-old John Kriban sat down on the steps and cried. "I had hoped all the time he'd get better," he said.

Upon the death of her beloved husband, Claire Ruth received messages of condolences from all over the nation. One came from Garden City, Long Island, and it read simply, "Deeply sorry.–Johnny Sylvester."[121]

Babe was not the first player from the 1926 Yankees team to pass away. He had been preceded by Miller Huggins, Urban Shocker, Tony Lazzeri, Herb Pennock and Lou Gehrig.

On August 19, 1948, neither the rain nor the steamy heat could keep the crowds from lining up along Fifth Avenue for a ten-block stretch from Forty-seventh to Fifty-seventh Streets, flanking New York City's St. Patrick's Cathedral. The majority of the seventy-five thousand people who came out that day were under the age of fifteen. And it was the kids who for days

John D. Sylvester and his wife Marita leaving the University Chapel Funeral Home in New York City on August 19, 1948, after paying their last respects to Babe Ruth. New York Daily News.

The funeral of Babe Ruth in St. Patrick's Cathedral, New York City, on August 19, 1948. Sitting in the Cathedral are Johnny Sylvester and his wife Marita. *Bettmann/CORBIS.*

and months before had gathered outside Memorial Hospital on East Sixty-eighth Street to support their idol in his neediest of times. Now they came and watched in utter reverence and silence as a highly polished mahogany coffin adorned with American Beauty roses and orchids was carried up the marble steps of the giant cathedral—a coffin containing the remains of the greatest baseball player and friend to kids the world had ever seen—Babe Ruth.

The coffin was followed by Ruth's widow Claire and his two daughters, Dorothy and Julia, and their husbands.

The guests inside St. Patrick's included the high and the mighty. New York Governor Thomas E. Dewey—who less than two months before had been nominated in Philadelphia as the Republican Party's candidate for president of the United States—was an honorary pallbearer, as was New York City Mayor William O'Dwyer. President Truman had already sent his condolences, as had former President Herbert Hoover. Mayor James M. Curley of Boston arrived with his son George, and also present was Baltimore Mayor Thomas D'Alessandro Jr. From the world of sports there were Connie Mack, Waite Hoyt, Joe DiMaggio, Moe Berg and Jack Dempsey.

The day was so hot that Babe's former teammate and another honorary pallbearer, "Jumpin Joe" Dugan, was quoted as saying, "I'd give a hundred dollars for a beer," to which former pitcher Waite Hoyt replied, "So would the Babe."

Also in attendance were the superb sportswriters who had glorified the Big Bam: Dan Daniel, John Drebinger, Frank Graham, James Kahn, John Kieran, Max Kase, Dan Parker, Jimmy Powers, Rud Rennie, Burris Jenkins and columnists Westbrook Pegler and Ed Sullivan.

The service was presided over by His Eminence Francis Cardinal Spellman, who was assisted by forty-four Roman Catholic priests and twelve altar boys.

Inside the mammoth gothic cathedral, thousands were seated, with hundreds standing in the naves. It was the largest funeral of the century up until that time, apart from that of President Franklin Delano Roosevelt. Of the over six thousands guests inside was one particular man—age thirty-three, a former submarine commander, a Princeton University graduate and now businessman who had an engraved invitation to sit front and center. His name was Johnny Sylvester.

The service lasted less than one hour. After the service, the funeral procession traveled north up Fifth Avenue, through the Bronx and past "the House that Ruth Built" for a final farewell.

The procession reached Gate of Heaven Cemetery in Hawthorne, New York, and George Herman Ruth Jr., age fifty-three, was laid to rest.

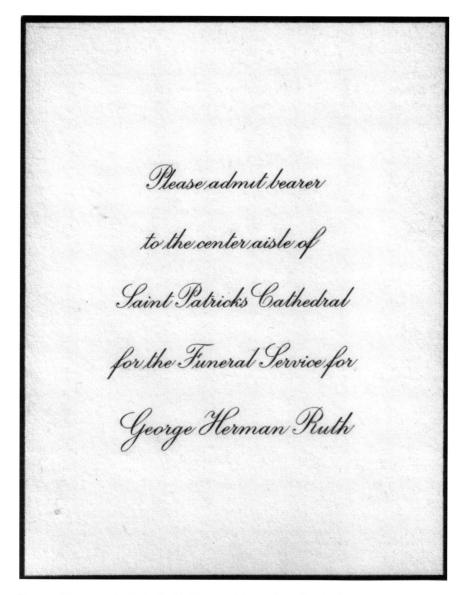

Engraved invitation for Babe Ruth's Funeral. *Johnny Sylvester Scrapbook.*

In all likelihood, pinned to Ruth's clothes was a small medal from a little boy from Jersey City, New Jersey, that had been sent to him when he was at French Hospital in New York in 1946. It was accompanied by a letter that read:

> *Dear Babe,*
> *Everybody in the seventh grade class is pulling and praying for you.*
> *I am enclosing a medal which if you wear it will make you better.*
> *Your pal–*
> *Mike Quinlan*
> *P.S. I know this will be your 61st homer. You'll hit it.*

Ruth wore that medal every day and vowed to wear it at his grave.[122]

The Babe's final resting place was a grave located less than two hundred yards from the grave of former Mayor Jimmy Walker. In the winter of 1926, Walker had cautioned Babe to "never let those poor kids down." Babe never did.

Prior to Ruth's death, a tribute to him had been planned to coincide with the annual Hearst Sandlot Classic baseball game sponsored by the *New York Journal American*. After his death, it was decided to turn the tribute into a memorial service prior to the game. Johnny Sylvester was invited to be one of the featured speakers.

On August 26, 1948, on one of the hottest nights in the history of the Polo Grounds, over thirty-five thousand people came out to the Hearst Classic dedicated to the memory of the Babe.

The proceedings commenced with the singing of the "Star Spangled Banner" by Metropolitan opera soprano Annamary Dickey. Then Steve Ellis, a radio sportscaster, introduced Bill Corum, a *New York Journal American* sports columnist, as the master of ceremonies. New York City Mayor William O'Dwyer addressed the crowd, followed by Joe DiMaggio, who received thunderous applause when he said, "Babe Ruth was my inspiration. It is one of my great regrets that I came too late to play alongside the Babe."[123] Musical highlights included Metropolitan opera baritone Robert Merrill singing "My Buddy," and a particular crowd pleaser was the twenty-two singers from the Police Athletic Choral who sang "Auld Lang Syne" and "Take Me Out to the Ballgame."

Comedy came in the form of Al Schact, who hilariously recreated Ruth's called shot of 1932, and comedian Joe E. Brown.

Ford Frick, president of the National League and a former *New York Journal American* sportswriter who had traveled with the Babe, gave his reminiscences.

Then Johnny Sylvester spoke and told the crowd how much he had appreciated what Ruth had done for him. He related the story of Ruth's

The Gilbert Paper Company of Menasha, Wisconsin, used this advertisement depicting a version of the story of Babe Ruth and Johnny Sylvester. It was later reproduced and circulated by the Babe Ruth Foundation. *Author's collection.*

visit to his home in Essex Fells, New Jersey, and said that Ruth brought him a baseball that had been one of his home runs in the 1926 World Series. Johnny would later say that it was the only time he "spoke to 30,000 people" and he would comment that it was difficult using the public address system at the Polo Grounds since after speaking his voice would reverberate back to him.[124]

The *New York Journal American* would sum up the event the next day as a grand pageant in which "Mayor O'Dwyer, Joe E. Brown and Johnny Sylvester—old friends of the Babe's—paid their tributes in heartfelt terms."[125] The paper also printed a large photograph of comedian Joe E. Brown hamming it up with Johnny Sylvester.

Johnny and Marita had one son, John Dale Sylvester Jr., born on September 1, 1949. When John Jr. was seven and eight years old, Johnny coached his Little League team. During the winter months, Johnny would return to his hockey playing and participate in pickup games on the local pond. John Jr. was sent to camp in Maine for five years, where Johnny and Marita would visit on long weekends.

The story of Babe Ruth and Johnny Sylvester became commercialized when an advertisement for the Gilbert Paper Company of Menasha, Wisconsin, ran an advertisement featuring Babe and Johnny in the May 1952 edition of *Fortune* magazine. The Babe Ruth Foundation would later reproduce the ad and make it a part of their *Legends of Babe Ruth* during the 1950s.

In 1951, Johnny purchased a charming colonial home in Garden City, Long Island. He continued to engage in the machinery sales and manufacturing business. He became president of Amscomatic, Inc. While at the company, Johnny would turn his talents to inventing new types of packaging machines.

On July 10, 1984, John D. Sylvester was granted patent No. 4,458,803 for a "Packaging Conveyor for Cylindrical Articles." This invention related to a conveyor belt that would carry cylindrical objects such as cups in an upright position and then have a pusher mechanism dispense them in orderly manner.

During the 1970s, Marita was plagued with medical problems. She suffered from periodic depression, had a pinned ankle and went through bypass surgery in 1978. In July of 1981, after a thirteen-month bout with lung cancer, she passed away.

Following the death of Marita Sylvester, Johnny and his son purchased a twenty-eight-foot Pearson Triton class fiberglass sailboat that had been built in 1961. They christened it the *Marita*. They moored it in Greenport, New

Johnny Sylvester at the helm of *Marita*, his Triton sailboat. *Courtesy of Ted Keenan.*

York, on the northern fork of the eastern end of Long Island. Father and son would sail on weekends during the fall and summer months in Peconic Bay and Fischers Island Sound. Every summer they would sail the boat to Martha's Vineyard and pick up Joe Hazen, a former editor of *Time-Life* books who had been Johnny's roommate at Princeton during his sophomore year, and the three of them would sail the Cape. Johnny often took his beloved dog Jill along. Johnny was a "salty sailor" and never flustered at the helm when his sailboat hit rough seas.[126]

On October 13, 1984, John Dale Sylvester Jr. married Edwina Scarsella of Cold Spring Harbor, New York. In 1985, Johnny Sylvester became a grandfather when John Jr. and Edwina gave birth to a baby girl named Sara Marita Sylvester on March 26.

On April 23, 1985, patent No. 4,512,464 was granted to John D. Sylvester for a "Method of Folding T-shirts and Folded Shirt Arrangement Resulting Therefrom." This invention related to the folding of t-shirts in a manner that would combine two or three shirts with a stiffener board and provide a proper display for marketing purposes.

In March of 1986, when Johnny was seventy years old, he was interviewed by Brian Sobel for an article entitled "The True Story of Babe Ruth's Famous Visit to Ailing Youth" that appeared in the March 1968 edition of

Johnny Sylvester as the doting grandfather with granddaughter Sara Marita Sylvester, who was born on March 26, 1985. He would live to enjoy three grandchildren. *Courtesy of Ted Keenan.*

Baseball Digest.[127] The article was one of the more truthful renditions of the Babe Ruth–Johnny Sylvester story but it, like many of the past versions, was not free from error. Sobel wrote that "a staff member" from National City Company made the contact with the Cardinals and the Yankees for the autographed balls, that Red Grange had delivered his football personally and that when Ruth went to visit Johnny he was "on his way to a baseball game for handicapped children and that Tilden's racquet had been used to win a Wimbledon championship."[128] Sobel did get Johnny to reflect back on his unique experiences and say, "I just look back on the events as a rare experience for a kid. Also, it proved most clearly to me that professional athletes, even one as great as Babe Ruth, are human too."[129]

In 1987, Johnny Sylvester was invited to be a guest speaker at the Babe Ruth Museum in Baltimore, Maryland, for a celebration of the 1927 Yankees. Johnny was joined at the time by Babe Ruth's sister and sports memorabilia collector Barry Halper. After the ceremonies, Johnny told John Eisenberg of the *Baltimore Sun*, "If I can enhance the memory of Babe, I'm happy to do it. He was a fantastic ballplayer. What he did for me, maybe it was done for publicity, I don't know. He did a good thing for me."[130]

John Dale Sylvester would become a grandfather again on February 24, 1988, with the birth of Emily Katherine Sylvester and once more on August 19, 1990, when Patrick Sylvester was born. After Amscomatic, Inc. was sold he continued working part time as a consultant to the new owners.

Johnny Sylvester died of natural causes on January 8, 1994. He was laid to rest next to his childhood sweetheart and beloved wife Marita in the Westview Cemetery in Westfield, New Jersey.

He left behind in his home in Garden City, New York, his scrapbook that he had started when he was eleven years old and a beautifully colored taxidermic macaw named Charlie.

This "orange crate label" was created by California artist Ben Sakoguchi, who states that "to form the core of my 'Unauthorized History of Baseball' series of paintings, I looked for icons (Babe Ruth) and compelling stories ('this one's for Johnny') that have made baseball such a part of the American social fabric." During the time that Johnny Sylvester was serving in the Pacific, three-year-old Sakoguchi was interned with his parents by the United States government at an internment camp in Poston, Arizona, simply because of their Japanese ancestry. *Courtesy of Ben Sakoguchi.*

Epilogue

After more than eighty years, the story of Babe Ruth and Johnny Sylvester remains one of the most popular and heartwarming in all of sports. In 1926, a young life was in jeopardy and there were no miracle drugs, there were no antibiotics—there was only a man, bigger than life, who connected with kids and brought excitement, hope and prolonged life to one eleven-year-old boy in Essex Fells, New Jersey.

And in the twenty-first century, this legendary story continues to be told and retold. It remains a powerful story and one that has captured the imagination and artistic talents of two very different individuals.

Artist Ben Sakoguchi was born in 1938 in San Bernadino, California. When he was but a few years old, Ben and his parents were interned by the United States government in a facility in Poston, Arizona, simply because of their Japanese ancestry. This ordeal did not deter Ben from allowing his art to glorify America's pastime and its icons.

After the war, Ben's parents were allowed to go back to running a small grocery store. Ben was fascinated by the brightly colored labels that were on the ends of the wooden crates used to ship oranges to market. In the 1970s, Ben noticed the labels at local flea markets and decided to recreate them as an art form. In 2006, he created a series of labels as part of his "The Unauthorized History of Baseball" series displayed during the "Winter Ball" exhibition at Los Angeles City College. He used his art to capture a great American story.

Dan Bern's father was a Jewish concert pianist who immigrated to Palestine from Lithuania, and his mother was a German poet and singer. His parents came to America and eventually settled in Mount Vernon, Iowa. There, in America's heartland, being raised by Old World parents, Dan learned to love music, songwriting and baseball. Dan Bern picked up *The Babe Ruth Story* as a boy and was hooked by its opening line: "I was a bad kid." Bern, who is often compared to Bob Dylan, recognized the mutual heroism in what the Babe and Johnny Sylvester did for each other. The result was this song:

"Johnny Sylvester Comes Back to Visit the Babe"
By Dan Bern

He looked like an apparition
Like a ghost without the sheet
But his eyes burned like a stove pipe
As he limped along the street

He walked by me slow but firmly
I knew he wouldn't stop to chat
But I thought that I might help him
He shook his head and touched his hat

He said I've come to see The Babe
They say Babe Ruth is dyin'
I've come to lift his spirits
Just like he once lifted mine
I can't promise any homers
I'm no Sultan of Swat
But I'll be up there swingin'
With everything I got

Years ago I lay in bed
My life hung like a rope
My sickly frame was wracked with pain
They said there was no hope

But the big guy would have none of that
He just sneered at tragedy
He hit four home runs that series
And each one was for me

Thanks to those arcing wallops
My wretched body healed
Thanks to the greatest player
That ever took the field

And as he stood above me
My eyes alert but dim
I never thought that someday
I'd be staring down at him

And I've come to see The Babe
They say Babe Ruth is dyin'
I've come to life his spirits
Just like he once lifted mine
I can't promise any homers
I'm no Sultan of Swat
But I'll be up there swingin'
With everything I got

Before there was Paul Bunyan
Before Old Honest Abe
Before there was John Henry
There always was The Babe
He took a hundred million spirits
And said Dare to be a land
He took one dying child
And said Stand up and be a man

And I've come to see the Babe
They say Babe Ruth is dyin'
I've come to lift his spirits
Just like he once lifted mine
I can't promise any homers
I'm no Sultan of Swat
But I'll be up there swingin'
With everything I got.

As for the principal players and managers from the 1926 World Series, they are forever enshrined in the National Baseball Hall of Fame in Cooperstown, New York:

1926 YANKEES HALL OF FAMERS

Plaques of members of the 1926 American League Champion New York Yankees who were inducted into the National Baseball Hall of Fame in Cooperstown, New York. *Center*: Manager Miller James Huggins; *clockwise*: George Herman (Babe) Ruth, Anthony Michael Lazzeri, Earle Bryan Combs, Herbert J. (Herb) Pennock, Waite Charles Hoyt and Henry Louis Gehrig.

As plans were developing for the centennial of baseball in 1939, Ford Christopher Frick, president of the National League and a former ghostwriter for Babe Ruth asked, "How about a Hall of Fame?" The idea was immediately adopted, with the first elections in 1936 and the first plaques hung in December 1937. Babe Ruth was in the first class of inductees. *National Baseball Hall of Fame Library, Cooperstown, New York. Layout by Kenny Evans.*

1926 CARDINALS HALL OF FAMERS

Plaques of the players from the 1926 World Champion St. Louis Cardinals who were inducted into the National Baseball Hall of Fame in Cooperstown, New York. *Center*: Player-Manager Rogers Hornsby; *clockwise*: Charles James Hafey, Jesse Joseph (Pop) Haines, James LeRoy Bottomley and Grover Cleveland Alexander. Other inductees who were involved in the 1926 World Series were Branch Rickey, who was in the Cardinals' back office in 1926 and responsible for creating the farm system, and Commissioner of Baseball Kenesaw Mountain Landis, who signed the players' checks and of whom it was said "ruled everything in baseball except the weather." *National Baseball Hall of Fame Library, Cooperstown, New York. Layout by Kenny Evans.*

Notes

Chapter One

1. *New York Star*, August 25, 1948.
2. *New York Times*, May 21, 1926.
3. Lieb, *Baseball as I Have Known It*, 153.
4. Lieb, *The St. Louis Cardinals*, 109–10.
5. Dickson, *The Dickson Baseball Dictionary*.
6. Jenkinson, *The Year Babe Ruth Hit 104 Home Runs*, 67.
7. Hoyt, *Babe Ruth as I Knew Him*.
8. Cook, *Waite Hoyt*, 61.
9. Kavanagh, *O'Pete*, 9.
10. *New York Times*, June 14, 1926.
11. Ibid., June 12, 1926.
12. Ibid.
13. Smith, *Babe Ruth's America*.
14. Ibid.
15. *Sporting News*, October 7, 1926, 2.
16. Ibid., 1.

Chapter Two

17. Reisler, *Guys, Dolls and Curveballs: Damon Runyon on Baseball*, 56–59.
18. *St. Louis Post Dispatch*, October 1, 1926, 22.
19. Ibid.
20. Smith, *Babe Ruth's America*, 179.
21. *New York Times*, October 4, 1926, 1.
22. Ruth and Considine, *The Babe Ruth Story*,145.
23. Ibid.
24. *Christian Science Monitor*, October 6, 1926, p. 14.
25. Lieb, *The Story of A Great Baseball Club*.
26. *St. Louis Post Dispatch*, October 5, 1926, 7
27. *New York Times*, October 5, 1926.

28. *Caldwell Progress*, October 8, 1926.

29. *Time*, March 5, 1934.

30. *Caldwell Progress*, October 8, 1926, 1.

31. Light, *The Cultural Encyclopedia of Baseball*.

32. Cunningham, *Boston Post*, October 9, 1926.

33. *New York Times*, October 6, 1926, 16.

34. Ibid.

35. *St. Louis Post-Dispatch*, October 6, 1926, 20.

36. Ibid.

37. Logbook of Charles A. Lindbergh.

38. *New York Herald Tribune*, October 7, 1926, 1.

39. *St. Louis Post-Dispatch*, October 6, 1926, 2.

40. Jenkison, *The Year Babe Ruth Hit 104 Home Runs*, 338.

41. Durocher, *Nice Guys Finish Last*.

42. *New York Times*, October 1926.

43. Jenkinson, *The Year Babe Ruth Hit 104 Home Runs*, 338.

44. *St. Louis Post-Dispatch*, October 7, 1926, 2.

45. Ruth and Considine, *The Babe Ruth Story*, 146.

46. *New York World*, October 7, 1926, 9.

47. Reisler, *Guys, Dolls and Curveballs: Damon Runyon on Baseball*, 211–12.

48. Ibid.

49. Ibid.

50. *New York Sun*, October 7, 1926.

51. Johnny Sylvester Scrapbook.

52. Ibid.

53. Ibid.

54. Ibid.

55. *New York Times*, January 29, 1991.

56. *Washington Post*, October 10, 1926, M12.

57. *New York Evening Post*, October 9, 1926.

58. Johnny Sylvester Scrapbook.

59. *Chicago Daily Tribune*, October 9, 1926, 21.

60. Lieb, *The St. Louis Cardinals*, 123.

61. *New York Times*, October 10, 1926, 1.

62. Jenkinson, *The Year Babe Ruth Hit 104 Home Runs*, 339.

63. Hornsby, *My War with Baseball*, 193.

64. Ibid.

65. Hornsby, *My War with Baseball*, 195–96.

66. Eig, *Luckiest Man*, 79.

67. Hornsby, *My War with Baseball*, 192.

68. Stewart, *Babe Ruth: A Biography*, 77.

69. *New York Times*, October 11, 1926, 1.

70. Ruth and Considine, *The Babe Ruth Story*, 150.

71. Ibid.

72. Montville, *The Big Bam*, 236.

Chapter Three

73. *New York World*, October 12, 1926, 1.

74. *New York Daily News*, October 12, 1926, 3.

75. Ruth Sylvester Elliott interview.

76. Johnny Sylvester interview with Ted Keenan.

77. Gallico, *Farewell to Sports*, 48.

78. *New York Daily News*, October 12, 1926, 3.

79. *New York Times*, October 12, 1926.

80. Ruth Sylvester Elliott interview

81. *Newark Evening News*, October 12, 1926, 1.

82. *Newark Star-Eagle*, October 12, 1926.

83. *Newark Evening News*, October 12, 1926, 1.

84. Ibid.

85. *Chicago Daily Tribune*, October 13, 1926, 23.

86 *Time*, October 18, 1926.

87. Cavanagh, *Ol' Pete*.

88. Sobel, "The True Story of Babe Ruth's Visit to Ailing Youth," *Baseball Digest*, 84

89. *Chicago Tribune*, October 12, 1926, 29.

90. Ibid.

91. Ibid.

92. *New York Times*, October 13, 1926.

93. *Caldwell Progress*, October 22, 1926.

94. *New York Times*, October 31, 1926.

95. Smelser, *The Life that Ruth Built*, 336.

96. Johnny Sylvester Scrapbook.

97. Lieb, *Baseball as I Have Known It*, 161

98. Ibid.

99. Fleming, *Murderers' Row*, 78.

100. Gallico, *The Golden People*, 44–45.

101. Lieb, *Baseball as I Have known It*, 161.

102. Ruth and Considine, *The Babe Ruth Story*, 171.

Chapter Four

103. Cobb and Stump, *My Life in Baseball*, 250.

104. *New York Times*, April 13, 1926, 1.

105. Weldon, *Babe Ruth*, 168–69.

106. *Sporting News*, April 1948.

107. *New York Times*, October 10, 1928.

108. *Ye Yeare Book* of Montclair Academy, 76–78.

109. Archibald Macleish, "Port of New York Authority," *Fortune*, September 1933, 119.

110. *New York Times*, July 26, 1929.

111. *Caldwell Progress*, February 8, 1941, 8.

112. *New York Times*, March 2, 1933, 9.

113. Ibid., March 22, 1933, 1.

114. *Wall Street Journal*, November 2, 1936, 4.

115. Jenkinson, *The Year Babe Ruth Hit 104 Home Runs*, 338.

116. *Caldwell Progress*, February 8, 1941, 8.

Chapter Five

117. John Dale Sylvester Jr. interview.

118. Johnny Sylvester Scrapbook.

119. Sobel, "The True Story of Babe Ruth's Famous Visit to Ailing Youth," *Baseball Digest*, 84.

120. Ruth and Considine, *The Babe Ruth Story*, 11.

121. Johnny Sylvester Scrapbook.

122. Ruth, *Guideposts Magazine*, October 1948.

123. *New York Journal American*, August 27, 1948, 22.

124. Johnny Sylvester interview with Ted Keenan.

125. Ibid.

126. Interview with Ted Keenan, May 23, 2007.

127. Sobel, "The True Story of Babe Ruth's Famous Visit to Ailing Youth," *Baseball Digest*, March 1968.

128. Ibid., 83, 84.

129. Ibid., 84

130. *Los Angeles Times*, August 7, 1987.

Bibliography

BOOKS

Allen, Frederick Lewis. *Only Yesterday: An Informal History of the 1920's.* New York: First Perennial Classics edition, 2000.

Berg, A. Scott. *Lindbergh.* New York: G.P. Putnam & Sons, 1998.

Breslin, Jimmy. *Damon Runyon: A Life.* Boston: Ticknor and Fields, 1991.

Carroll, John M. *Red Grange and the Rise of Modern Football.* Urbana-Champaign: University of Illinois, 2004.

Cavanaugh, Jack. *Tunney: Boxing's Brainiest Champ and His Upset of the Great Jack Dempsey.* New York: Random House, 2006.

Cobb, Ty, with Al Stump. *My Life in Baseball.* Lincoln and London: University of Nebraska Press, 1993.

Conner, Floyd. *Baseball's Most Wanted II, The Top 10 Book of More Bad Hops, Screwball Players, and Other Oddities.* Washington, D.C.: Brasseys, Inc., 2003

Cook, William A. *Waite Hoyt: A Biography of the Yankees' Schoolboy Wonder.* Jefferson, NC: McFarland & Company, Inc., 1944.

Creamer, Robert W. *Babe: The Legend Comes to Life.* New York: Penguin Books, 1974.

D'Amore, Jonathan. *Rogers Hornsby: A Biography.* Westport, CT: Greenwood Press, 2004.

Bibliography

Deford, Frank. *Big Bill Tilden: His Triumphs and the Tragedy.* Toronto:Sport Media Publishing, Inc., 2004.

Dickson, Paul. *The Dickson Baseball Dictionary*. Facts on File, 1989.

Doig, James W. *Empire on the Hudson: Entrepreneurial Vision and Political Power at the Port of New York Authority.* New York: Columbia University Press, 2001.

Durocher, Leo. *Nice Guys Finish Last.* New York: Simon & Schuster, 1975.

Eig, Jonathan. *Luckiest Man: The Life and Death of Lou Gehrig.* New York: Simon & Schuster Paperbacks, 2005.

Eisenberg, Lisa. *The Story of Babe Ruth: Baseball's Greatest Legend.* Chicago: Gareth Stevens Publishing, 1997.

Fischer, Margaret Jane. *Calvin Coolidge, Jr. 1908–1924.* Chicago: Academy Books, 1981.

Fleming, G.H. *Murderers' Row.* William Morrison & Company, 1985.

Frick, Ford. *Games, Asterisks, and People: Memories of a Lucky Fan.* New York: Crown, 1973.

Gallico, Paul. *Farewell to Sport.* New York: Knopf, 1938.

———. *The Golden People.* New York: Doubleday, 1964.

Gilbert, Brother. *Young Babe Ruth: His Early Life and Baseball Career from the Memoirs of a Xaverian Brother,* Edited by Harry Rothberge. Jefferson, NC: McFarland and Company, 1999.

Gilbert, Thomas. *The Soaring Twenties: Babe Ruth and the Home-Run Decade.* London: Franklin Watts, 1996.

Grange, Harold E., and Ira Morton. *The Galloping Ghost: The Autobiography of Red Grange as told to Ira Morton.* Wheaton, IL: DuPage Heritage Gallery, 1953.

Green, Louise Tuthill. *Shelter Island.* Charleston, SC: Arcadia Publishing Co., 1997.

Greenberg, David. *Calvin Coolidge.* New York: Times Books, 2006.

Holtzman, Jerome. *No Cheering in the Press Box.* Austin: Holt, Rhinehart & Winston, 1973.

Honig, Donald. *Baseball America: The Heroes of the Game and the Times of Their Glory.* (Barnes and Noble, Inc., 1997.) Originally published by Scribner, 1985.

Hornsby, Rogers, and Bill Surface. *My War with Baseball.* New York: Coward-McCann, Inc., 1962.

Hoyt, Waite. *Babe Ruth as I Knew Him.* New York: Dell Publishing Co., 1948.

Jenkinson, Bill. *The Year Babe Ruth Hit 104 Home Runs.* New York: Carroll and Graf, 2007.

Kyvig, David E. *Daily Life in the United States, 1920–1940.* Chicago: Ivan R. Dee, 2002.

Levenson, Barry. *The Seventh Game: The 35 World Series That Have Gone the Distance.* New York: McGraw Hill, 2004.

Lieb, Fred. *Baseball as I Have Known It.* (Bison Books, The University of Nebraska Press, 1996.) Originally Published by G.P. Putnam's Sons, 1977.

Lieb, Frederick G. *The St. Louis Cardinals: The Story of a Great Baseball Club.* New York: G.P. Putnam, 1944.

Light, Jonathan Fraser. *The Cultural Encyclopedia of Baseball*, 2nd Ed. Jefferson, NC: McFarland & Company, 2005.

Luisi, Vincent. *New York Yankees: The First 25 Years.* Charleston, SC: Arcadia Publishing Co., 2002.

Meaney, Tom. *Babe Ruth: The Big Moments of the Big Fellow*. New York: A.S. Barnes and Company, 1947.

Mercer, Paul. *Babe Ruth*. Barnes and Noble Publishing, 2003.

Miller, Nathan. *New World Coming: The 1920's and the Making of Modern America*. DaCapo Press, 2003.

Montville, Leigh. *The Big Bam: The Life and Times of Babe Ruth*. New York: Doubleday, 2006.

Nicholson, Lois P. *Babe Ruth: Sultan of Swat*. Goodwood Press, 1994.

Okrent, Daniel, and Steve Wulf. *Baseball Anecdotes*. New York: Harper & Row Publishers, Inc., 1989.

Robinson, Ray. *Iron Horse: Lou Gehrig in His Times*. New York: W.W. Norton & Company, Inc., 1990.

Reisler, Jim. *Babe Ruth Slept Here: The Baseball Landmarks of New York City*. South Bend, IN: Diamond Communications, Inc., 1999.

————, ed. *Guys, Dolls and Curveballs. Damon Runyon on Baseball*. New York: Carroll and Graf, 2005.

Robertson, John G. *The Babe Chases 60: That Fabulous 1927 Season, Home Run by Home Run*. Jefferson, NC: McFarland & Company, Inc., 1999.

Ruth, Babe, as told to Bob Considine. *The Babe Ruth Story*. New York: Scholastic Book Services, 1967.

Sanford, William R., and Carl R. Green. *Babe Ruth*. New York: Macmillan Publishing Company, 1992.

Smelser, Marshall. *The Life that Ruth Built*. Lincoln: University of Nebraska Press. 1975.

Smith, Robert. *Babe Ruth's America*. New York: Thomas Y. Crowell, 1974.

Snyder, John. *Cardinals Journal: Year by Year & Day by Day with the St. Louis Cardinals Since 1882*. Cincinnati: Emmis, 2006.

Sobel, Ken. *Babe Ruth and the American Dream*. New York: Random House, 1974.

Sobel, Robert. *Coolidge: An American Enigma*. Washington, D.C.: Regnery Publishing, 1998.

Spatz, Lyle, ed. *The SABR Baseball List & Record Book: Baseball's Most Fascinating Records and Unusual Statistics*. New York: Scribner, 2007.

Stevens, Julia Ruth, with Bill Gilbert. *Major League Dad: A Daughter's Cherished Memories*. Chicago: Triumph Books, 2001.

Stewart, Wayne. *Babe Ruth: A Biography*. Greenwood Press, 2006.

Treadwell, Theodore R. *Splinter Fleet: The Wooden Subchasers of World War II*. Annapolis, MD: Naval Institute Press, 2000.

Votano, Paul. *Tony Lazzeri: A Baseball Biography*. Jefferson, NC: McFarland & Company, 2005.

Wagenheim, Kal. *Babe Ruth: His Life & Legend*. First e-reads publication, 1990.

Walsh, Christy. *Adios to Ghosts*. New York, 1937.

Weldon, Martin. *Babe Ruth*. New York: Kessinger Publishing, 1948.

ARTICLES

Frick, Ford, and Frank Graham. "Baseball's Greatest Dramas: Alex Fans Lazzeri." *New York Journal American*, March 21, 1961.

Ruth, George Herman. "The Kids Can't Take It If We Don't Give It!" (Babe Ruth's Last Message) *Guideposts* magazine, October 1948.

Sobel, Brian. "The True Story of Babe Ruth's Famous Visit to Ailing Youth." *Baseball Digest*, March 1986

Periodicals

Boston Post
Caldwell Progress
Chicago Daily Tribune
Christian Science Monitor
Guideposts Magazine
Kansas City Star
Los Angeles Times
New York Daily News
New York Evening Post
New York Journal-American
New York Star
New York Sun
New York Times
New York World
Newark Evening News
Newark Star-Eagle
Sporting News
St. Louis Post Dispatch
Time
Washington Post

Year Books, Scrapbooks and Log Books

Johnny Sylvester Scrapbook.
Logbook of Charles A. Lindbergh, Missouri Historical Society.
Ye Yeare Book of Montclair Academy, 1932.

Interviews

Dan Bern, May 23, 2007.
John Dale Sylvester Jr., May 5, 2007.
Julia Ruth Stevens, December 9, 2006.
Recording of taped interview of April 1989, of Johnny Sylvester by second cousin Ted Keenan.
Robert Bush, July 2, 2007.
Ruth Sylvester Elliott, May 17, 2007.
Ted Keenan, May 27, 2007.

Index

A

Abbe, Charles S. 96
Alamac Hotel 72
Alexander, Grover Cleveland 24, 25,
    27, 46, 49, 56, 69, 72, 75, 107,
    109, 143
Algonquin Hotel 91, 92, 95
Amscomatic, Inc. 134
Associated Press 27, 64, 69, 97

B

Babe Comes Home, The 97, 126
Babe Ruth Story, The 37, 103, 139
Baldwin, Samuel W. 111
Baltimore Orioles 126
Bancroft, Dave 16
Barrett, Edward F. 111
Barrow, Ed 78
Bascom, Henry 58
Batten, Barton, Durstine & Osborn,
    Inc. 126
Bay Head, New Jersey 36
Beals, Lennie 104
Bell, Herman 62
Bell, Lester 62, 65
Bendix, William 126
Berg, Moe 130
Bern, Dan 139
Bloody Angle 47
Bluege, Ossie 51
Borden, Frank C., Jr 85
Boston Braves 20, 102

Boston College 115
Boston Herald 69
Boston Post 56, 64, 85
Boston Red Sox 21, 24
Bottomley, Jim 45, 65, 143
Bradley Beach, New Jersey 81, 85, 88
Brann, Louis J. 116
Brice, Fanny 97
Bronx, New York 40
Brooklyn Royal Colored Giants 85
Brown, Harriman & Co. 116
Brown, Joe E. 132
Buckley, George D. 50, 97
Burns, George 28

C

Caldwell Progress 64, 65
Camiskey, Charles 27
Cavalcade of America 126
Chase Hotel 28
Chicago Bears 67
Christian Science Monitor 48
Citizens' Military Training Camps 26
Cleveland Indians 16, 28
Clough, Edgar 40
Cobb, Ty 16, 105, 106
Cochrane, Mickey 105
Combs, Earle 19, 47, 62
Corum, Bill 132
Cunningham, Bill 51, 56, 64
Cuno, Wilhem 105
Curley, James M. 130

Index

D

D'Alessandro, Thomas 130
Daniel, Dan 130
Dark Chapter, The 95
Dempsey, Jack 16, 44, 130
Dewey, Thomas E. 130
Dickey, Annamary 132
DiMaggio, Joe 132
Douthit, Taylor 45
Drebinger, John 130
Dugan, Joe 26, 62, 66
Dunn, Jack 126
Durocher, Leo 58, 103

E

Eberle, Gertrude 16
Ellis, Steve 132
Essex Fells, New Jersey 36, 42, 64, 81,
    85, 87, 96, 109, 126, 134, 139
Evening World 65, 66, 88

F

Fairmount Park Racetrack 72
Falkenburg, Jinx 122
Fenway Park 21, 116
Fields, Marshall, III 122
Fields, W.C. 97
Flanagan, Reverend E.J. 24
Frazee, Harry 24
Frick, Ford 102, 132, 142

G

Gallico, Paul 83, 92, 103
Galvin, John F. 112
Gates of Heaven Cemetery 130
Gehrig, Lou 21, 42, 45, 46, 51, 66, 74,
    78, 88, 89
Gilbert Paper Company 133, 134
Globe-Democrat 49
Graham, Frank 47, 130
Grange, Red 16, 44, 69, 84, 92
Grove, Lefty 105

H

Haenigsen, Harry W. 88, 94
Hafey, Chick 62, 65, 143
Haggerty, Frank 126, 127
Haines, Jesse 27, 51, 74, 143
Haley, Martin J. 49
Halper, Barry 137
Halsey, N.W. Company 33, 114
Harriman, Ripley & Co. 116
Harris, Bucky 20
Harrison, James R. 66, 106, 109
Henderson, Ray 42, 81
Hildebrand, George 75
Hitching Post 121, 122
Hoover, Herbert 130
Hornsby, Mary Dallas 32
Hornsby, Rogers 38, 48, 49, 64, 66,
    71, 72, 78, 81, 143
Houston, Charles (Mike) 104
Hoyt, Waite 21, 26, 58, 64, 74, 107,
    130, 142
Huggins, Miller 20, 21, 26, 65, 66,
    127, 142

I

Illinois 44, 45, 67, 72, 119

J

Jenkins, Burris 130
Jolson, Al 97
Jones, Bobby 16

K

Kahn, James 130
Kase, Max 130
Keenan, Helen 33
Keith Academy 126
Kellogg, Elenore 81
Kennett Square 26, 65
Kieran, John 130
Kingsley School 109
Knight, Doc 26
Koenig, Mark 21, 66, 74, 97

Index

L

LaHiff, Billy
  speakeasy 75
Lambert, Major Albert Bond 47, 57
Lambert Field 57, 106
Latham, Arlie 27
Lazzeri, Tony 21, 40, 46, 47, 75, 76,
  95, 97, 142
Lenglen, Suxanne 44
Liberty Bell 15
Lieb, Fred 16, 102, 103
Lipton, Thomas 105
London Times 44
Lowenstein, Robert 85

M

Mack, Connie 105, 130
Madison Square Garden 45
Mantle, Mickey 36
Maris, Roger 104
McGovern, Artie 16, 17
McGraw, John 24, 40
McNamee, Graham 42, 79
Meany, Tom 23, 103, 122
Merrill, Robert 132
Meusel, Bob 21, 66, 78, 102
Miller, Victor 48
Mitchell, Charles E. 110, 114
Mitchell Field 26
Mona Lisa 15
Montclair Academy 109, 112
Montclair High School 33
Mount Vernon 15
Mueller, Heine 24
Murderers' Row 19, 21
Murray, Marita 121

N

National Baseball Hall of Fame and
  Museum 14, 104, 142, 143
National City Bank 33, 111, 112
National City Company 33, 50, 57,
  110, 111, 116
National League 16, 27, 109
Newark Evening News 64

Newark Star-Eagle 64, 84
Newspaper PM 122
New York Daily News 81, 83, 85, 103
New York Giants 24, 32
New York Herald Tribune 57, 88
New York Star 122
New York Times 26, 42, 44, 46, 64, 66,
  83, 112, 116
New York World 81
New York Yankees (baseball) 36, 67,
  92, 106, 107, 126
New York Yankees (football) 67, 92
North Caldwell 110, 116

O

O'Dwyer, William 130, 134
O'Farrell, Bob 27, 66, 78
Olvany, George V. 112
Oriell, Miss 83
Orton, George W. 50
osteomyelitis 36

P

Pantages, Alexander 97
Pantages circuit 97
Pashcal, Ben 66
Pecora, Ferdinand 111
Pegler, Westbrook 16, 130
Pennock, Herb 21, 45, 65, 66
Philadelphia 15, 16, 26, 44, 50, 92,
  103, 130
Philadelphia Athletics 105, 106
Philadelphia Municipal Stadium 15
Pinehurst, North Carolina 106
Poland, Bernard V. 85
Polo Grounds 24, 89, 132
Port of New York Authority 110
Powers, Jimmy 130
Princeton University 104, 112, 130
Pyle, Charles C. "Cash and Carry"
  44, 67

Q

Queen Marie of Rumania 97
Quinlan, Mike 132

Index

R

Ramsey, John E. 111, 112
Rath, E.J. 95
Readers Digest Radio Edition 121
Rennie, Rud 130
Rentschler, Gordon S. 112, 114
Rhem, Flint 27, 58
Richards, Vincent 44
Rickard, George "Tex" 44
Rickey, Branch 16, 24, 45
Robertson Aircraft Corporation 57
Rommel, Eddie 105
Roosevelt, Franklin D. 130
Ruether, "Dutch" 51
Runyon, Damon 62, 75
Ruppert, Jacob Colonel 42, 46, 105
Ruth, Claire 123, 127

S

Sakoguchi, Ben 139
Sands, Alexander H., Jr. 110
Savage, Courtney 95
Scarsella, Edwina 135
Schact, Al 132
Sesqui-Centennial Exposition 15, 50
Shawkey, Bob 51, 69
Shelter Island 33
Sherdel, Bill 27, 45, 65, 109
Shocker, Urban 21, 46
Sisler, George 20
Smith, Ken 104
Southern Pines, North Carolina 106
Speaker, Tris 16
Sporting News 21, 27, 107
Sportsman's Park 49, 50, 58, 65, 106, 109
St. Louis Browns 20, 27, 28, 46, 50
St. Louis Cardinals 16, 24, 25, 27, 28,
        32, 40, 45, 46, 47, 48, 50, 51,
        56, 58, 60, 63, 65, 66, 72, 75,
        81, 82, 107, 143
St. Louis Post-Dispatch 49, 56, 62
St. Patrick's Cathedral 127
Sulgrave Manor 15

Sullivan, Ed 130
Sylvester, Emily Katherine 137
Sylvester, Horace C., Jr. 33, 34, 36, 50,
        57, 110, 111, 112, 114, 116, 118
Sylvester, John D., Jr. 134, 135
Sylvester, Nathaniel 33
Sylvester, Patrick 137
Sylvester, Sara Marita 135, 136

T

Thevenow, Tommy 47
They All Want Something Coming 95
Thomas, Myles 51
Tilden, William Tatem, II 90, 91, 92,
        93, 94, 95, 96
Truman, Harry S. 130
Tryon, Eddie 92
Tunney, Gene 16, 44, 46

U

U.S. National Tennis Championships 92
USS *Prairie State* 119

V

Vidmer, Richard 27, 46, 72

W

Walberg, Rube 105
Walker, Jimmy 42, 105, 106, 132
Walsh, Christy 81, 85, 102
Walters, Bucky 56
Wells Motor Car Company 60
Westview Cemetery 137
Wilmer, Rae 122
Wilson, Jimmie 109

Y

Yankee Stadium 16, 40, 44, 50, 105, 130

Z

Zachary, Tom 104, 109

About the Author

Charlie Poekel is a former member of the New Jersey State Historical Commission, having been twice appointed by Governor Christine Todd Whitman. He currently serves on the Board of Managers of the Sons of the Revolution, which owns the Fraunces Tavern Museum in New York City. He is a trustee of the Elisha Kent Kane Historical Society, chairman of the Essex Fells, New Jersey History Committee and is a member of the Society for American Baseball Research.

In 1976 he was honored by the U.S. Chamber of Commerce as an Outstanding Young Man of America.

He holds a BA degree from the George Washington University and a JD degree from the Washington College of Law of the American University. He is a practicing attorney and a member of the Bar in New York, New Jersey and the District of Columbia.

Charlie Poekel is the author of *West Essex* and a contributing author to the *Encyclopedia of New Jersey*.

He is married to the former Lynn Giordano. They have three children—Charles III, Will and Patty—and they divide their time between homes in Manhattan, Essex Fells, New Jersey, and Marion, Massachusetts.

Please visit us at
www.historypress.net